Gymnastics

Systematic Training for Jumping Horses

Compass Points for Riders

Gymnastics

Systematic Training for Jumping Horses

James C. Wofford

COMPASS EQUESTRIAN
Henley-in-Arden

Edited by Valerie Wofford Watson

Design: Alan Hamp
Line drawings: Maggie Raynor

Front cover photograph by kind permission of Charles Mann.

British Library Cataloguing in Publication Data
A catalogue record for this book
is available from the British Library

ISBN 1 900 667 21 5

Published in Great Britain in 2001 by
Compass Equestrian Limited
Cadborough Farm, Oldberrow
Henley-in-Arden, Warwickshire, B95 5NX.

Printed in England
by Westway Offset Limited, Luton

Contents

Acknowledgements

Any book on training horses is derivative, and this one is no exception. Therefore I should acknowledge some of the influences on this book.

My family has been involved with horses for over 80 years now, and the influence of my father and mother on my attitudes towards horses is unmistakable. I grew up in a family where my father, both brothers, and one sister-in-law had ridden in the Olympics, and one cousin was a champion steeplechase jockey. Combine a family background such as this with a young man who had an insatiable appetite for learning about horses, and sooner or later a book like this is going to pop up.

While I have been fortunate to have studied under many trainers during my career , the two who have had the greatest influence on my thinking are Bertalan de Neméthy and Jack LeGoff .

At the same time no one learns everything they know about horses from one source. I am lucky to have been surrounded throughout my life by horses of all shapes, sizes and ability, and from each one who has passed through my life, I have learned something. That process continues to this day.

Bill Steinkraus has been generous enough to read and comment on various manuscripts that I have developed over the years. While I am forever indebted to him for his help with this book, the inevitable transgressions of grammar and colourful syntax that have crept into this book are mine alone.

Sharon Anthony and Kevin Freeman read this book at an early stage, and they now appreciate the meaning of the term 'rough draft'. Their suggestions were invaluable.

My long-suffering wife Gail deserves especial thanks for putting up with my absent-minded behaviour while I was writing this book, and far more besides. My children, and their respective spouses, view my condition with an amused tolerance for which I am eternally grateful.

My work has been illuminated, as well as illustrated, by my

talented illustrator Maggie Raynor. When you see her illustrations, you will literally see what I mean.

This book would never have come to fruition without the help and support of my editor, Valerie Wofford Watson. Thank you for thinking of me, Valerie.

But in the final analysis, this book's main influence is my late brother, Warren, who always thought there would be time for him to write it himself.

Jim Wofford
Fox Covert, Upperville, Virginia
May, 2001

List of Illustrations

Which Gymnastic?
A brief synopsis

Key to Gymnastic Exercises

The exercises discussed in this book have all been reproduced in diagrammatic form showing:
a) the distances and shape of the fences in each exercise and
b) the sequence in which it should be jumped.
Distances are noted in metric and imperial measurement.

The symbols used are as follows:

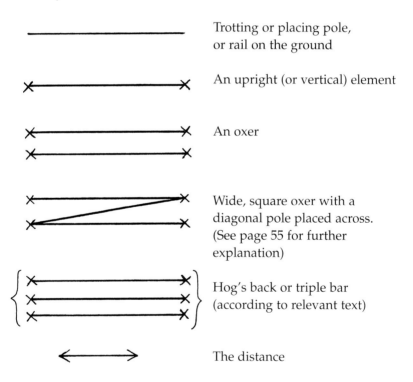

Trotting or placing pole, or rail on the ground

An upright (or vertical) element

An oxer

Wide, square oxer with a diagonal pole placed across. (See page 55 for further explanation)

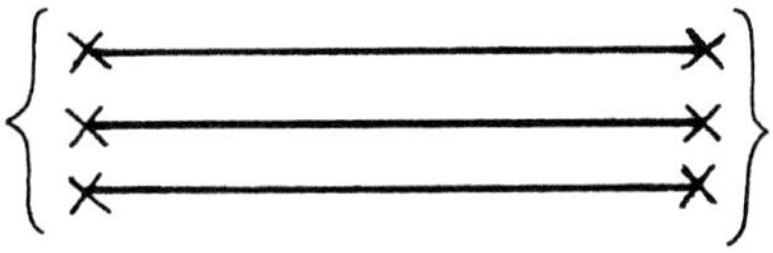

Hog's back or triple bar (according to relevant text)

The distance

Symbols for sequences are as follows:

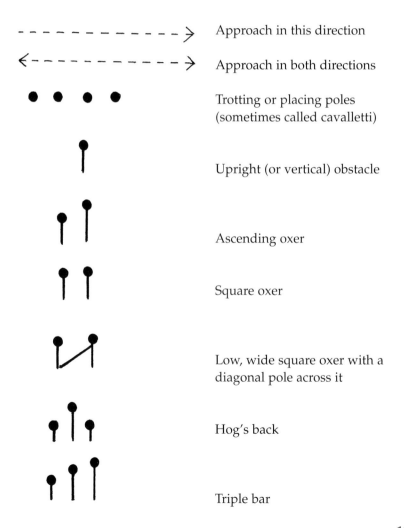

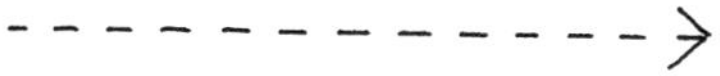 Approach in this direction

 Approach in both directions

 Trotting or placing poles (sometimes called cavalletti)

 Upright (or vertical) obstacle

 Ascending oxer

 Square oxer

 Low, wide square oxer with a diagonal pole across it

 Hog's back

 Triple bar

Fig 1. The horse who begins with the most basic of jumping skills will be able to progress through gymnastic work.

Introduction

Gymnastic jumping is the best tool available to improve your horse's performance. It has existed for nearly 100 years. However, anyone interested in training their horse to date, has had to consult a number of books on the subject, picking up a little bit here and a little bit there. While most of the great riders and trainers I have known over the last 30 years have used these techniques, until now it has been difficult to find a single source book on the topic.

Most of my adult life has been spent teaching horses and riders to jump. Indeed, it has been a rare U.S. team at the Olympics or World Championships that has not had at least one of my students on it. At the recent Olympics in Sydney, all four U.S. team members, including the individual gold medallist, were graduates of my programme. I hope you will agree that this system of training has withstood the ultimate test... it works in the real world!

What you will find in this book are a series of gymnastic exercises which will improve the way your horse jumps. These exercises are designed to lead you and your horse step-by-step from simple, low exercises for young, inexperienced horses, to very difficult, complex exercises for talented, experienced horses.

You will also find chapters on selecting a horse (the more suitable your horse is the better your results will be), and the rider's position; (there is an inescapable connection between how well you ride, and how well your horse goes).

Regardless of your horse's talent and experience, you will find an exercise in this book that will make him a better jumper. At the same time, these exercises are designed to be systematic and progressive. If you practise over some of the easier exercises first, then the more complicated exercises will make more sense to you and your horse when you attempt them.

Every horse is born knowing how to jump. However, when you put the weight of a rider on the horse's back, it will take a lengthy training process before that horse can reach his full potential. A regimen of these gymnastic exercises will improve you and your horse's :

- ❑ Balance
- ❑ Technique
- ❑ Flexibility
- ❑ Confidence
- ❑ Fitness

I use the term ***gymnastic jumping*** to mean placing any two or more obstacles a certain distance apart. This distance will then determine the number and length of your horse's stride or strides between the obstacles. By first repeating and then later varying the gymnastic exercises,your horse's performance will be much improved. The final results will be so rewarding and beneficial that you will be pleased you undertook the process.

You will find this book useful as a tool for either the continued training of your horse, or his remedial education. While it can certainly be read cover-to-cover, you can also use this book as a reference. Have a rushing problem? Need a new jump lay out and you are not sure what to build, or what distances to use between obstacles? Have a horse who runs out? I have some ideas. Just check in the quick reference section, ***Which Gymnastic?*** on page 10. It will steer you in the right direction.

However you decide to use it, I am sure you will find something in this book that will improve your horse, which is the true horseman's highest goal.

1

The Horse

If you are going to jump your horse, you might as well have one who has the right talent and physique. I prefer horses that measure between 15.3 and 16.1hhands. Obviously there have been successful horses of every size and shape, but in my opinion horses within this range tend to be the most balanced and athletic, and certainly balance and athleticism are key ingredients in the making of a good jumper.

It is not theoretically correct, but when evaluating a horse, the first thing I do is 'look him in the eye'. My ideal horse is the horse that I fall in love with again every morning when I see his face hanging over the stable door, looking for breakfast. If you do not like a horse the first time you see him, do not talk yourself into buying him. You will always be secretly unhappy with him and you won't make the necessary excuses for his inevitable mistakes during the training process.

I prefer horses that are slightly higher at their withers than at their croup. In general, the lower fronted the horse is, the more skill you will need in order to present him in balance to an obstacle. If you are going to participate in activities in which speed will play a part, such as hunting, point-to-pointing, or eventing, then you will want a horse that tends to keep its own balance.

Working from the ground up, the horse should have four normal, well shaped feet , at least of a size in proportion to the horse's overall body weight. The forelegs should form two parallel lines when viewed from the front. The hind legs should form a vertical line from the point of the hock to the ground. If the hind legs do not form this straight line, they should be set slightly under the body, rather than set behind. There are certain conformation flaws that I can accept in a prospective purchase. If the horse is slightly 'over' at the knee, it is often the sign of a horse that will snap his knees in the air over a fence. But a horse who is 'behind' in his knees is so prone to injury that I will pass him by.

If a horse is cow-hocked, or sickle-hocked, I think this concentrates his power under the body. But if his hocks are set wide, or even worse, set wide and behind the body, don't buy him. You will never get him to engage, and he will always run on his forehand.

Make sure to take into account the temperament of the horse, and its suitability for you. If you weigh 200lb and are ham-fisted, do not buy a sensitive, 15.3 hh chestnut Thoroughbred mare. If you are a bit timid, you will need a horse that does not take a lot of kicking to get to the other side. When you buy a horse, buy one that is not only a good jumper, but one that suits you as well.

It goes without saying that when choosing a prospect, the quality of all three paces are important. However, if the horse is being selected for show jumping only, pay the most attention to the canter, which should be smooth and balanced. Some roundness in the show jumper's action is desirable. The walk and trot of the show jumper can be given less attention. Horses being evaluated for foxhunting and eventing should be correct in all three paces. While racehorses need only to gallop, it is no secret that correct biomechanics lead to soundness, balance, and long-term usefulness. Usually, the better the walk, the better the gallop, as they are both four-beat gaits. Watch the horse walk at liberty, and you will get a better idea of his potential to gallop and jump.

If you are going to purchase a prospect that has never been taught to jump, find a horse of the type that I have described above. If it has a lovely flowing four-beat walk that is straight, smooth and energetic, then you have probably found a horse that will be able to gallop and jump. The most consistent indicator of jumping ability I have ever found is prominent withers. A horse with prominent withers, built slightly uphill, and with 'the look of eagles' is a good prospect.

The horse must be able to see the obstacle in order to jump it, yet it is so obvious that people forget to take this into account. In the pre-purchase examination make sure that your veterinarian pays

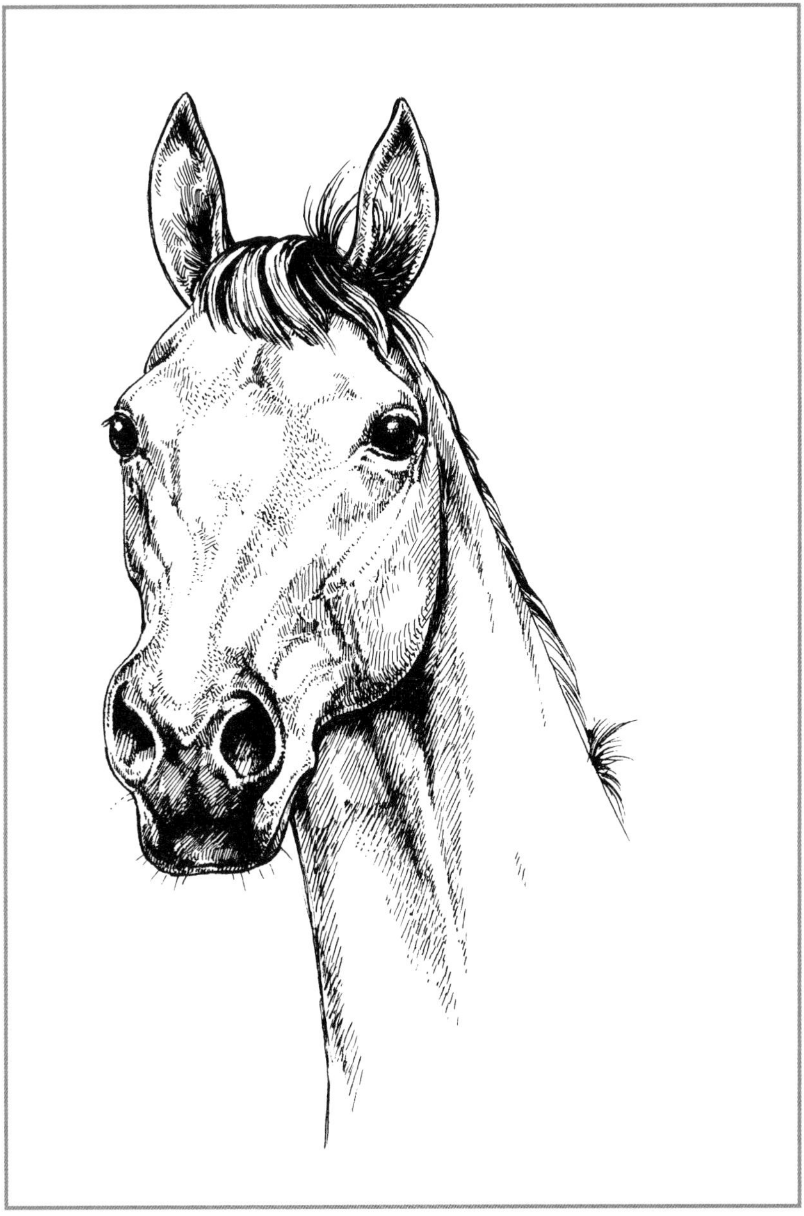

Fig 2. The look of eagles.

Fig 3. The horse's field of vision.

particular attention to the vision of the horse. In addition, during the training of the horse it is important that you understand how a horse looks at the obstacle.

The horse has monocular vision. This means that he sees with a fixed field of focus. This field is approximately ten degrees in front of the plane of his nose. In other words, for the horse to see obstacles farther ahead in his path he must lift his head and neck and point his nose farther along the line of this approach.

This fact immediately tells us that all of our efforts to bring a horse 'round' to the jump are wrong, if by 'round' we emphasise only the flexion of the horse at the poll, and ignore the engagement of the hindquarters. Allow your horse to approach the obstacle with a comfortable outline, and direct your efforts towards approaching the obstacle with your horse 'on the contact', not 'on the bit'. As long as your horse carries his poll higher than his withers, he has enough balance and engagement to jump up to 4ft (1.2m).

How a Horse Jumps

If you are going to teach your horse to jump, it is important that you know how horses jump. Whether from the trot or the canter your horse begins his jumping motion with his forehand. He will lower his head and neck slightly, plant both front feet, and then bring his head and neck back and up to begin his jumping motion. As his forehand leaves the ground his hindquarters will reach forward under his body and propel him along the arc that his forehand has started to produce.

In theory the horse should describe a perfect half-circle in the air with its body. This arc is referred to somewhat inaccurately as the 'bascule', a French term, from the verb which means to rock or swing. The shape of the bascule will be largely governed by the take-off point. In theory the horse's take-off should be the height of the fence away from the fence. He should reach the high point of his bascule over the highest point of the fence, and land the height of the fence beyond the fence. Once we know the shape of the perfect jump, we can start to analyse the flaws in our horse's jumping technique as we go through our training programme.

At the same time, we should not be blinded by theory. Over small obstacles in the real world, both the take-off and the landing points are usually farther away from the obstacle than the height of that obstacle.

Use your knowledge of theory to measure your horse's performance. For example, the horse's jump will be what we call 'flat' if the approach speed has been too great for the size and shape of the jump, or if the take-off point has been too far away from the first rail of the obstacle. If the arc of the jump starts too close to the obstacle, forming a square outline, we call it 'sticky', 'chipping in' or sometimes 'putting in a short one'. This shape is usually caused by a horse getting behind your leg at the point of take-off or by taking off too close to the jump.

Once you have analysed the shape of your horse's arc and compared it in your mind with the perfect arc that you are trying to produce, the corrections that you should make become more obvious. For example, if your horse is jumping too flat, slow him down. If your horse is sticky over his obstacles, bring him to the fence at a more forward rhythm and close your legs more strongly at the point of take-off. These habits are easier to correct by using a series of gymnastic obstacles than by working over individual obstacles, because you know the number of strides before the next obstacle and, thus, the

Fig 4a. A horse jumping flat.

Fig 4b. A horse jumping sticky.

take-off point when you arrive at the obstacle. If you have limited experience jumping, be sure to have someone more knowledgeable watching. It can be difficult to analyse your horse's performance whilst you are also concentrating on not falling off.

Fig 4c. A horse jumping just right.

The horse's jump can be divided into five phases. These are:

- **Approach**
- **Take-off**
- **Flight**
- **Landing**
- **Departure**

If your horse's shape in the air over the obstacle is incorrect, it is usually because something has gone wrong either in the approach or the take-off. Occasionally during gymnastic jumping, the second obstacle of a series will cause problems because, for example, the rider has toppled back in the air over the first obstacle, or has fallen forward against the horse's neck during the landing and departure. Remember that the departure from the first obstacle in a line of gymnastic obstacles is the approach to the next. By their very nature gymnastic jumps are set in relation one to another.

While dressage as such lies outside the scope of this book, I should point out that the improvement of your horse's performance over obstacles is going to be directly related to the quality of your horse's dressage training. The calmness, balance, engagement and strength that your horse will gain by a concerted effort to improve his dressage work will directly affect his performance over obstacles. Each time you get a new horse to work with, you must place as much emphasis on his training on the flat as you do on his work over fences.

2

The Rider

Position

The best way to improve your horse's jumping is to improve your own position. In order to find the correct jumping position you must adjust your stirrup leathers correctly. To do this, sit in the saddle at the halt and take both feet out of the stirrups. Then let your legs hang straight down, and adjust the stirrup leather until the tread of the stirrup touches the inside of your leg at, or just above, your ankle bone.

Place both feet in the stirrups with the ball of your foot on the tread of the stirrup. Press enough weight into your ankles so that your heels are lower than your toes. The sensation you should have is that the weight moves from the inside of your leg into your heel. An onlooker should see about a 90 degree angle behind your knee, after you have adjusted your stirrups.

Viewed from the front, your feet should form a slight angle away from the line of the horse's body. This angle varies from rider to rider. In general, it should approximate the extent to which your feet turn when you walk. For example, if you toe out slightly at the walk, your feet should turn away from the horse to about the same degree. If you are pigeon-toed at the walk, your feet will stay more nearly parallel to the horse's body. However, at no time should you attempt to force your lower leg into a position that is not comfortable for your joints. For your purposes, natural and supple should be synonymous words.

I will occasionally refer to a two-point position, or a light three-point so I need to explain my terminology. For example, when I mention a two-point position, I am referring to the two points of contact between your knees and the saddle.

Fig 5. Rider in two point position.

Your weight should be supported by your knees and ankles, and your buttocks should not touch the saddle. The grip point is more towards the back of the knee than towards the kneecap.

This is the position you should use when:

- **galloping**
- **jumping**
- **in posting (rising) trot**
- **you want to take your weight off your horse's back**

Because of the importance of your two-point position, I am going to give you a couple of exercises to strengthen and improve that position.

The first exercise is to post without stirrups. This is an excellent exercise to develop and strengthen the muscles you will need to gallop and jump. If you can rise at the trot without stirrups for five minutes, you are probably fit enough for competitive activities.

The second exercise is to keep your stirrups, assume the two-point position, and stay suspended over your horse's back at the trot and the canter. Press your weight down into your ankles, and practise absorbing the shock of your horse's movement with your knees, not with your hips. Your stirrup leather should remain vertical throughout this exercise. Keep your hands off your horse's neck, your back slightly arched, and your head and eyes forward. This exercise will help to improve your jumping position.

Another position I will refer to I call the 'light three-point'. While keeping the two points of contact behind your knees, you should close your knee angle and allow your weight to settle back into the saddle. The weight of your body is now supported by three points – your two seat bones and your pubic bone. This position is called 'light' because your shoulders should be in front of your hips. The light three-point is used in the approach to obstacles. In a 'full' three-point , your shoulders would be over your hips, your stirrup leathers would be longer, and you would be in a dressage position.

While you cannot improve your horse's jumping without improving his dressage, that topic is outside the focus of this book.

When you are either in a two-point, or a light three-point position, the grip of your lower leg against the saddle should appear to be evenly distributed between the inside of the knee and the inside of the ankle. This grip can move up and down the leg as the situation dictates. If your horse tends to be sluggish in front of an obstacle, your grip must move lower in your leg towards the heel in order to urge him forward. If your horse 'cracks his back' over an obstacle or bucks on landing, your inside knee grip should be very strong.

If you make a mistake when jumping you should emphasise the grip of the knee rather than the grip of the heel. Although gripping with the knee may cause the lower leg to swing, at least it will help you to stay attached to the horse, and if you are attached to the horse you can improve. If you grip with your heels, however, the knee will come

Fig 6. Rider in light three point position.

away from the saddle and you will have the sensation of riding a greased pig. This is upsetting to your horse and can spoil both his landing and his departure from the obstacle. This will quickly lead to a downward learning curve.

Because you are often going to need to rise out of the saddle when riding, the inner surface of the thigh should not actually grip the saddle. However, the muscle on the outside of the thigh is very helpful in attaching you to the saddle and therefore to the horse.

Working our way up in your position , we arrive next at the hip and the small of the back. There should be a slight forward angle at your hip when you are seated with jumping length stirrups. The small of your back should show a slight forward arch at your waist, your back should be flat, shoulders square, head erect and your eyes looking straight ahead through your horse's ears.

Once you have assumed the correct position with your upper body, adjust the reins so that the inside point of your elbow is just in front of the point of your hip. Then form a straight line from your elbow to your hand, and through the reins to the horse's mouth.

Hold your reins as if you were carrying a plate of soup. This means that your thumbs should be on top of the reins and your hands should remain the width of your horse's mouth apart. Maintain this relationship both on a straight line and on turns or circles.

When the horse jumps maintain the straight line from your elbow to your horse's mouth. Notice that the more your horse bascules over a fence, the lower his mouth goes in relation to his withers, and therefore the lower down the neck your hand must travel in order to retain this classical straight line.

Fig 7. Position of the rider's hands in relation to the bascule of the horse.

When we speak of a rider who has 'good hands' over jumps, we actually mean that the rider has supple elbows and poised shoulders. The sensation you should have when following your horse's mouth is that you have an elastic tied to the back of your elbow, and your horse stretches this elastic forward and down. Take care not to suddenly increase or decrease this elastic contact.

Vision

In the approach to an obstacle keep your eyes focused on the top rail until it disappears between your horse's ears. The reason for this is that you will be able to predict your stride in front of the obstacle more accurately if you see the obstacle. We refer to this process as 'timing'.

Timing refers to the rider's ability to predict and influence the remaining increments of a stride in front of the obstacle. Your timing will immediately improve if you watch the obstacle in the approach. Look at the front rail of your oxers, look at the top rail of verticals, and look at the back rail of triple bars. You have probably been taught to look beyond the obstacle in the approach – I certainly was. However, if you watch the obstacle instead, you will find that it makes an immediate positive impact on your riding. Watching the obstacle may not produce instant accuracy, but it will produce instant harmony between you and your horse. Timing is a skill which will take time to develop. In the meantime, worry less about riding to a 'spot' in front of the jump and worry more about riding in a steady rhythm to the jump.

Equipment

Just as you should never jump without someone else in the area, you should never jump without a helmet. That helmet should fit correctly, and must have a harness strap that keeps it in place during a fall.

When training your horse in gymnastic jumping, use the mildest equipment possible. A plain, hollow-mouth or flat-ring snaffle and simple noseband should suffice. It may be that you have to use a stronger bit when at a competition, but as far as possible, try to use simple equipment at home and train your horse calmly and classically. This will give you the best possible chance to make lasting improvements in your horse's performance.

Saddles

First of all the saddle should fit the horse. Next, it should be suitable for jumping and comfortable for you. Find the low point of the saddle by sitting in it on the horse at the halt. Move back and forth along the gullet until you find the low point of the saddle. Then adjust your stirrup leathers as described earlier in this chapter. If the saddle fits you correctly, you should then find that your knees fit just behind the knee roll. I do not like saddles with a pronounced knee roll, as I find that they cause most riders' lower legs to swing backwards. The new close contact saddles seem to be the best for all round jumping.

Protective Boots

Your horse should use protective boots of some kind on all four legs. I prefer leather boots, with a foam lining, and strap and buckle closings. While for every-day use boots with velcro closings are sufficient, they tend to come undone in competition.

Full leather boots afford the best protection for eventers, racehorses, young horses and field hunters with less than good action, while show hunters and jumpers should use open-fronted boots. If your horse has any tendency at all to over-reach, he should always wear bell (over-reach) boots on his front feet when jumping.

Effects of Gymnastic Jumping on the Rider's Position

Gymnastic jumping will have an extremely beneficial effect on your position. There are several reasons for this:

❑ The predictability of the striding allows you to be prepared for the horse's jumping motion.

❑ You will be able to repeat the same exercise, making adjustments in your lower leg, upper body, and so on, in order to find the exact balance point over your horse at any time throughout the jumping effort.

❑ Gymnastic jumping will also improve your timing. Look at the next obstacle when landing over the preceding obstacle. Tell yourself that you are a certain number of strides away from the next obstacle and then ride to that obstacle in the correct rhythm and on the correct number of strides. This will help develop your 'eye for distance'.

- Exercise 5 on page 50 is of especial value when working on your own position.

3

Training Facilities

If you are going to train your horse to jump you are going to need a training area. The most important requisite of a jumping arena is good footing. The surface does not have to be of any particular material, but your horse should be able to make a hoof-print in the surface when moving normally around the arena. In order to determine this, walk out onto the surface of your training area and dig your heel into the surface slightly. You should be able to make a print in the surface. Another good rule of thumb is that, after your horse goes by, an onlooker should be able to see an outline of your horse's foot in the surface. There must be some displacement of the footing in order to absorb the concussion of jumping.

Landing areas should be suitable for jumping on to because repetition is part of learning. We want to repeat the effort where the footing is not going to give your horse a bad experience especially when jumping down, for example off banks. The repetitive nature of training horses to jump means a lot of wear and tear on the take-off and landing sites. This is especially true when jumping on wet ground. Be sure to repair the damage to the footing to ensure the best possible training conditions for your horse. Likewise, if the ground is hard, add shavings or some form of sand to the landing in order to maintain your horse's soundness and confidence.

It is of definite benefit to have your jumping area enclosed by a fence or a wall of some type. This will serve to make your horse concentrate better and is invaluable if you should happen to become disconnected from your horse, for whatever reason, during a training period. If your arena is outdoors make sure that the drainage is good enough for it to be usable in all but the most inclement weather conditions.

You must have a ground person present at all times when you are jumping; safety should never be far from your mind. In addition, having a person on the ground, especially one who can make knowledgeable observations about you and your horse's performance, is of great value. Besides the safety aspect, the ground person's role is to set the jumps, to add obstacles as the training grid progresses in difficulty, and to adjust the heights and spreads according to the horse's reaction. The ground person should be able to move obstacles, reset poles, and generally make themselves useful during the training period. It is extremely difficult to engage in any kind of gymnastic jumping if you have to dismount and reset obstacles yourself while you are trying to train your horse.

General Comments regarding the Gymnastic Exercises

As you progress through the training exercises described in this book keep these simple, yet important, guidelines in mind.

First of all, never worry that you have set the heights too low, especially early in the training session and most especially when schooling young or inexperienced horses. It is easy to raise the heights and increase the spreads later on as your horse gains confidence and experience, whereas if your horse loses confidence early in the session it is very difficult to re-establish his confidence.

As the exercises in this book become more technical, make sure to lower the height of the preceding jumps when you add the next obstacle. Once you explain the new exercise to your horse with the obstacles low, he will not be as bothered by height and spread when the time comes to increase them. Always finish your training session on a good note.

I have developed these exercises over a period of 30 years of doing clinics and they have been jumped safely by thousands of horses. Remember, however, that they were used in clinic or group lesson situations.You must be aware that every horse is different and you should use your common sense in adjusting the distances. If your horse takes an average stride and reacts in a normal fashion in jumping situations, you should find that these distances are comfortable for your horse. If your horse has an unusually long or short stride, by all means adjust the distances to suit your horse.

Measuring Distances

When setting distances, be very precise about the measurement between obstacles or between cavalletti and obstacles. When I use the term 'cavalletti', I mean poles laid on the ground at measured intervals.

Use a measuring tape to set the exercises, then practise pacing the distance between the obstacles. This will do two things:

- ❑ You will know that you are jumping an exercise that is set and measured correctly.
- ❑ Your step will become more accurate, which is a nice habit to have when you pace a combination at a competition.

There are already enough variables involved in the training of horses. Do not introduce more variables by being inaccurate with the measurement between the obstacles that you set up.

I am obsessive about setting up exercises symmetrically in the arena. When jumping more than one obstacle in a row, make the centre of the exercise parallel to the long side of the arena. You can do this by measuring from the first standard of your exercise to one wall and then from the last standard of the exercise to the same wall, making sure that you get the same distance at both the beginning and the end of the line.

If the distance is inconsistent and the line is skewed, you may teach your horse to jump more in one direction than another.

I like to see symmetrical cups, too, with all the pins facing the same way. A little time and effort taken in raking the footing will go a long way towards maintaining the base of your arena's footing, and maintaining your horse's soundness and enthusiasm for jumping.

I have used feet as a unit of measurement throughout this book. I understand that this is not terribly modern, but it is the way I was trained and I think in those units. However, for the convenience of those more modern, you will find metric measurements in brackets beside mine.

When measuring between cavalletti I measure the inside distance from one pole to another. When I measure canter cavalletti, I do the same. When placing jumps in sequence, I measure from the back rail of the last element to the first rail of the succeeding element. Remember to change the distance between elements when you change the spread of one of the oxers.

I have assumed that all of your rails are 12ft (3.6m) long. If this is not the case, remember to adjust the relationships when measuring distances between angled rails.

In order to ensure the safety of the situation, here are some basic guidelines:

- ❑ Always wear a helmet, with the chinstrap fastened.

- ❑ Do not jump alone.

- ❑ Do not jump on hard ground.

- ❑ Be careful to place your ground lines at least in the vertical plane of the front element and never behind. (Ground lines are not entirely necessary; and indeed they can be done away with once the horse gains some confidence in his jumping.)

- ❑ The ends of each rail resting in the jump cup should be at least one inch from the standard. Do not 'wedge' the standards. If your horse makes a mistake, the rail should come out of the cups.

- ❑ Always remove all cups from the standards when they are not in use. Your horse may cut himself on an open cup left on a standard, if he swerves, or 'drifts' down a series of obstacles.

When adding elements, the variation of the height and spread of

Gymnastic exercise 1

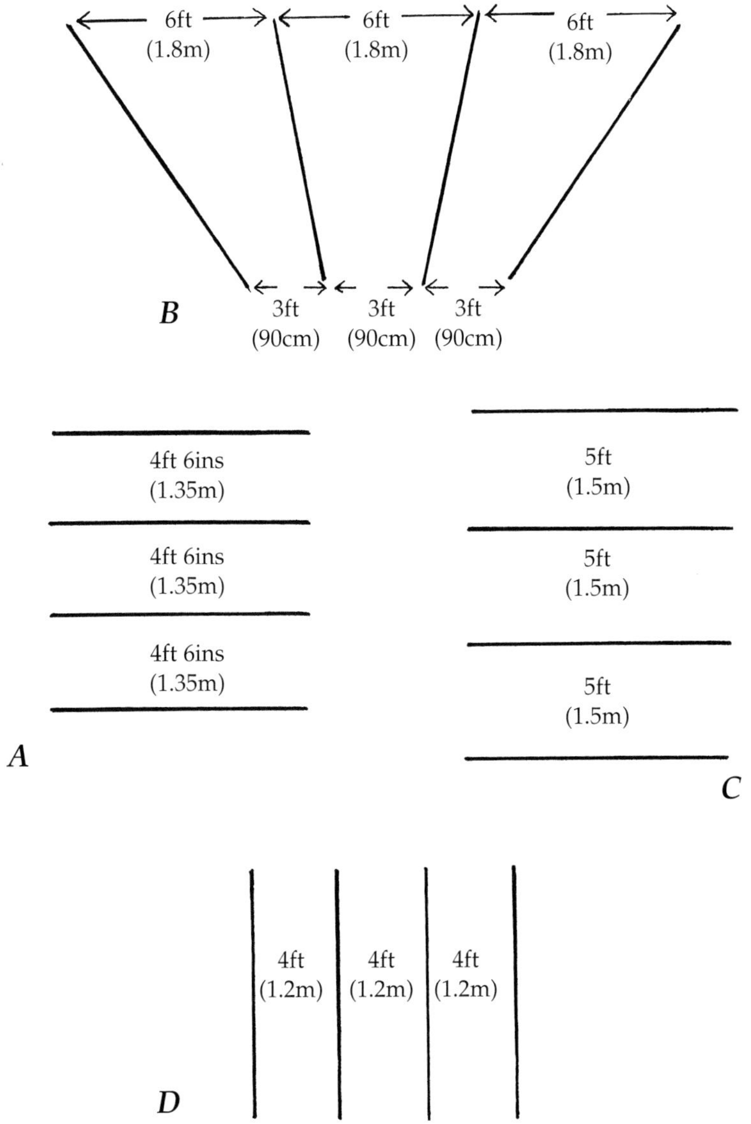

the obstacles is more important than the actual measurement. For example, verticals will look higher to your horse in a line of fences if the oxers are lower and wider.

A 12ins (30cm) variation from one obstacle to another is entirely acceptable and will cause your horse to concentrate and make a more accurate assessment of the situation.

Oxers will not have the required effect on your horse's bascule until they are at least as wide as they are high. Whenever schooling a young horse, set the initial heights low. Then introduce your horse to changes in height and spread by small, that is 3ins (7.5cm), graduated changes. Later on, more experienced horses should confront situations in which the first obstacle in the line is the highest and also situations in which there is an extreme variation in height and spread from one obstacle to another. You will make more progress if you jump your horse more times over lower obstacles than you will by attempting to jump fewer, larger obstacles in the training session.

4

Beginning Gymnastics

This chapter addresses the horse that has some jumping experience but has not been introduced to more technical aspects of the sport. Never forget that it is essential to maintain the calmness and confidence of your horse throughout his training over obstacles. If you preserve these two elements, you will be able to make the most rapid progress and produce the most long-lasting and beneficial effects on your horse.

Approach these exercises at a calm, regular, balanced pace with quite a long or possibly even loose contact. I place a great deal of emphasis on awakening the horse's initiative at an early stage of the horse's training and attempting to maintain that initiative throughout their career; thus, my emphasis on soft reins.

Do not ride your horse as if you must give him a 'good' ride, but rather attempt to be an intelligent passenger. Once your horse gets to the obstacle he must arrange his footwork and propel his body over the fence. At this point it is your job to stay out of his way. If you run into difficulties you should either lower the obstacle or, if you are jumping gymnastic obstacles in sequence, remove the last obstacle and lower the rest until you get your horse going forward again. Once he is calm and balanced, you can resume the exercise.

Your goals are for your horse to maintain his rhythm, balance and regularity of stride over obstacles. I think that we should teach our horse to balance himself, not to expect us to balance him. An excellent exercise is to count in rhythm with your horse's stride as he proceeds down the line of obstacles. For example, if you have obstacles set up to produce one stride in between them, then as the horse lands over the first element you should be able to say out loud 'land'. Then as your horse reaches the end of his stride before leaving the ground over the second obstacle you should be able to say 'one'. If there are succeeding obstacles you should be able to repeat this down the entire gymnastic line.

This sounds like an exceedingly simple exercise, but you will find it surprisingly difficult to perform correctly while your horse is jumping. You may find that the timing of your voice is not in rhythm with your horse's landing. This is the most common mistake that I see in my clinics when students attempt this exercise. Usually riders who make this mistake have some weakness in their jumping position, thus causing a loss of balance. This loss of balance is very distracting, because the rider will think more about self-preservation than about maintenance of balance and rhythm in the landing phase of the jump. If you land out of balance, it means there is something wrong with your position. If there is something wrong with your position, it is usually that your lower leg position is faulty. Most of the time, if you improve your lower leg position, you will improve your landing after jumps.

Your horse should maintain an absolutely steady regular cadence down the line of obstacles. Your counting should also be steady, regular, and cadenced. Riders who are nervous and who become agitated when they are jumping will find that their voices will increase in volume and pitch. Many riders will quicken the cadence of their counting until their voice and their horse's stride are no longer in synchrony. Many times this is the same rider who will blame his horse for rushing.

You can do exercise 1 in either a jumping or a dressage saddle. If you ride in a dressage saddle, you should shorten your stirrups one hole, because the added height of your horse's step over the poles will cause you to need a bit more stability than if you were riding just on the flat. For the rest of the exercises you will need a jumping saddle.

Practise keeping your eye on the next object in your horse's path. For example, if you are trotting towards a pole on the ground, look through the horse's ears at the pole until it goes out of sight. With young horses and inexperienced riders I do not ask the rider to alter the horse's step in front of the pole. I want to awaken the horse's initiative. Whether he takes a slightly long step or adds an additional step before the pole, I am equally satisfied. If he steps on the pole, the chances are good that he will learn from the experience and not do it again. If he continues to step on the poles on the ground, I suggest that you find another prospect, as this one is probably too dumb to make any improvement over obstacles.

Practise looking at each object in your horse's path even when there are additional objects. If you are trotting over a series of rails on the ground followed by an obstacle, look at the first rail on the ground, and then keep your eye on the obstacle until it goes out of sight between the horse's ears. This will help you maintain a straight line through the gymnastic exercises and will also help you develop your timing. You can't see your stride if you don't see the jump. So look at the jump until it goes out of sight between the horse's ears.

For all cavalletti work, and indeed all sorts of jumping work, your horse should wear protective boots or bandages on his legs as, especially when stepping over poles, he may knock his legs while learning to co-ordinate them.

These exercises rely on cavalletti to stabilise your horse's length of step, speed, and balance. If an obstacle follows the cavalletti, use the posting (rising) trot until your horse steps over the last pole, then softly lower your seat to the saddle. This will ensure that you are in touch with your horse's back when he leaves the ground.

Do not lean forward while you are negotiating the cavalletti. When your horse leaves the ground, you should have the sensation that he has brought his withers up towards your chest.

Gymnastic exercise 1 (page 37)

After you have warmed your horse up at the walk, trot and canter, then trot into the exercise marked **A** in the sketch. Cavalletti set at this distance will produce a working trot for most horses. These exercises are all designed for horses with some jumping experience. If your horse is extremely green he probably should not be attempting this exercise yet. However, if he is slightly inexperienced or is an experienced jumper but has not done much work over cavalletti you can pull the first and the third poles in towards the centre line of the arena. This will produce a 9ft (2.7m) distance between two poles. Horses find this exercise easier and will soon become stable and regular at the trot which is always your goal. You can then put the four poles together and work in both directions over four of them on the ground. After you have established your horse's balance and rhythm here you can proceed to the curved poles in **B.**

At the posting trot, proceed on a circle in either direction through **B**. Keep your horse's direction adjusted so that the length of his step on the curve feels the same as it did over **A**.

Once you and your horse have become adept at this you can then start to enter, for example, closer to the 3ft (90cm) end of the poles where the distance is shorter and then let the horse angle away from the centre of the circle. This will cause your horse to go from a working trot to a medium trot or possibly, if your angle becomes too great, even take a couple of steps of extended trot. If your horse takes two steps between the poles or breaks into a canter, you have probably asked too much flexibility from him. Aim closer to the 3ft (90cm) end of the curve, and enter **B** again at the posting trot.

Alternatively, you can enter from the outside of **B**, where the rails are farther apart. This will cause your horse to take quite a large step at first. Angle in towards the 3ft (90cm) distance between the last two poles. This will bring your horse back to a working trot or even a slightly collected trot. Having worked in both directions over **B**, including being able to angle both ways, you can then proceed to **C**.

The poles positioned at **C** will produce the sensation of extended trot and you may find that your horse cannot reach enough in his fourth step to get out over the last pole without 'chipping in' an additional step. Simply remove the last pole and continue. You will find that, after a couple of days work over cavalletti, your horse gets the message and you can replace the fourth pole. You should work in both directions over the 5ft (1.5m) poles at **C** until your horse can maintain his regularity and length of step. After a short break proceed to **D**.

These four rails on the ground, set at 4ft (1.2m) apart, will produce a collected trot. Although these exercises can be ridden either posting or sitting, you should definitely use rising trot until your horse becomes adjusted to them. Again, work both ways through **D** until your horse is relaxed and steady in his balance and rhythm. He should be able to deal with the rails without any interruption in the flow of his movement, changing only the length of his step to adapt to the various distances that you have put in his path.

After another break you can now link these four elements together in order to produce various transitions that will be of great benefit in teaching your horse to be flexible. For example, enter **A** on the right hand in a working trot, where the rails are 4ft 6ins (1.35m) apart. As you leave **A** turn right in such a fashion that you produce an arc through **B** which causes your horse to change the length of his step from working to collected trot. In other words you would enter exercise **B** from the outside in. This will put your horse in a slightly collected frame. Proceed directly then to **C**, which will produce an extended trot. After the extended trot at **C**, turn right and enter the shorter cavalletti at **D**.

If your horse has difficulty with this you can do **A**, **B**, and **C** as I have described and then in posting trot circle (or repeat a circle until your horse has settled down to working trot), turn and enter **D**, thus producing a collected trot. If you have successfully done this, walk, reward your horse and let him relax and consider his effort while you plan your next series of repetitions through these exercises. When you resume the posting trot, work in both directions and vary the relationship between the exercises to improve and confirm your horse's flexibility.

Take a moment to remind yourself of your horse's bad habits. If your horse tends to rush at the trot, he will not need too many applications of **C**. He should come from outside in rather from inside out at **B**, as this will cause him to continually re-balance and collect his step rather than rushing forward. If, on the other hand, your horse is choppy strided or lazy, a bit more emphasis on **C** and a few more repetitions at **B**, going from inside out, will teach him to lengthen his step. The total amount of exercise over these rails in any one period should not exceed 45 minutes, including the periods of rest between exercises.

These exercises will fit comfortably in a 75ft x 150ft (22.8m x 45.7m) arena.

Gymnastic exercise 2 (fold out pages 44 and 45)

Start this exercise with four rails on the ground set 4ft 6ins (1.35m) apart and one more rail 9ft (2.7m) away, so that you have five poles lying parallel on the ground. Trot back and forth several times to show your horse the distance between the poles and to establish his rhythm and balance. You can then raise the rail at **B** to produce a suitable warm-up fence. This will usually be 18–24 ins (45–60cm). You should now trot through the trotting poles towards the warm-up rail at **B**. Repeat this exercise several times.

As the horse becomes more experienced at cavalletti and gymnastic jumping, you can also raise the rail at **B**, keeping in mind that you should lower it back to its original height before adding further elements in the gymnastic line.

After you have warmed up over **A** and **B**, make sure that the first rail is put down to its initial height and then raise a second rail at **C** to about 2ft (60cm). This element should be 18ft (5.5m) from the first obstacle. This will produce an exercise of four trotting poles and two vertical obstacles. Again, trot in, jump the first obstacle as before, land, take one stride and jump out. After several repetitions, if your horse seems willing and comfortable, you may raise the rail at **C**. Keep in mind that the performance of your horse is the best judge of how rapidly you can progress in terms of raising the fences.

If this is your horse's first experience with gymnastic jumping, or he has limited experience with this type of training, then four to six repetitions through **A**, **B**, and **C** should be sufficient for your first training period. After an easy day of work on the flat you can come back and repeat this exercise. If your horse appears to understand what is being asked of him and especially if he maintains his calmness, balance and regularity through the exercise, then you can change **C** into an oxer. Make sure that the front rail of **C** is level or slightly lower than the back rail. You should then jump these two obstacles several times, entering the gymnastic at posting trot and cantering quietly through over the two obstacles. Jump the oxer at **C** several times before starting to raise it. I usually try to finish the series of repetitions with the last obstacle set at the size and spread that would be required at the horse's level of competition.

Gymnastic exercise 2
Sequence

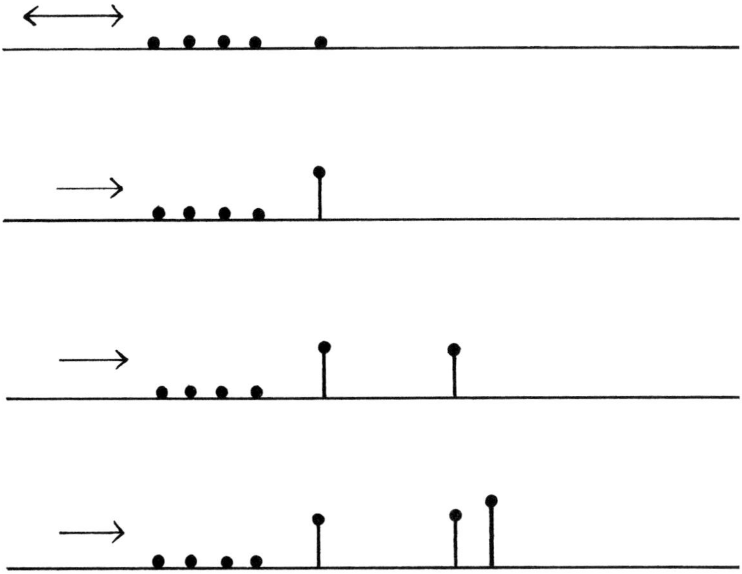

Gymnastic exercise 2

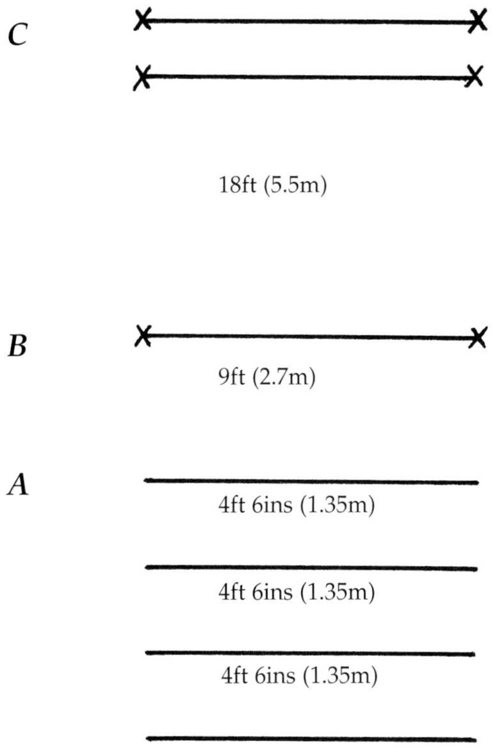

Departure

I should add a general comment here about the departure. Training your horse does not stop the instant your horse lands over the obstacle. You should have a plan for the departure, which will help you to re-establish your rhythm and balance.

Riders tend to land thinking about their performance over the first obstacle, rather than preparing their horses for the next obstacle. Remember that the departure from one obstacle is the approach to the next.

Gymnastic exercise 3 (fold out pages 48 and 49)

Exercise 3 is a continuation of the work that was done in exercise 2. Start again with the rails taken away from **B**, **C** and **D**, which will leave only the open standards, four trotting poles, and one rail on the ground at **B**. Warm your horse up as before. Work in both directions through the exercise. This will introduce variety into your horse's environment, and cause him to remain interested later on when you approach only from the cavalletti toward the obstacles.

Repeat the procedure for exercise 2 until you are jumping the obstacles at a comfortable height. If you have raised the obstacle at **B** to slightly higher than your usual level, you should lower that fence before adding a rail at **C**. For example, set the obstacles in the following manner. The first time that you confront the entire sequence of obstacles they should probably be 2ft (60cm) at **B**, 3ft (90cm) at **C** and 3ft 3ins (1m) at **D**, with **D** set as a vertical. Once your horse is calm and confident, you can make **D** into an oxer.

The only way you can be sure of the correct height is to observe very carefully your horse's reactions. It is up to you to determine the correct height for your horse's training. If he remains calm, balanced and attentive, you are on the right track. If he becomes agitated and starts rushing you should lower the obstacle or even remove the last obstacle in the line and continue working quietly and methodically until he re-establishes his mental and physical balance.

If you feel your horse losing confidence as the jumps get higher, you must immediately lower the obstacle and narrow the spread until your horse's confidence has returned.

The distance between the three obstacles will produce a one-stride from **B** to **C** and a one-stride from **C** to **D**. Remember to strive for balance and regularity. If your horse gets too close to **C** and/or **D** put a pole on the ground exactly half the distance between **B** and **C** and, again, between **C** and **D**. This will make your horse land sooner after **B**, thus giving him more distance in front of **C** to complete his stride, and the same from between **C** and **D**. Continue this exercise, gradually raising the heights and spreads as your horse develops fitness and displays regularity and balance through the exercise.

Gymnastic exercise 4 (fold out pages 48 and 49)

This exercise is a continuation of the previous exercises. Work as systematically through this exercise as you did in the preceding ones. In its final form the exercise will require your horse to trot the cavalletti, jump **B**, take one canter stride, jump **C**, take another canter stride, jump the oxer at **D**, land, take two strides and jump an additional oxer at the end of the line.

Do not add the next rail until you are sure the horse understands the problems posed by the one before. If you have raised one of the fences at **B**, **C** or **D** to a marked degree, make sure that you lower it before you add the next obstacle in the line. When you increase the technicality of an exercise, you should decrease the height and spread until you are sure that your horse understands what you want from him. For practical reasons, I rarely change the spread at **D**, because I would then have to change the distance to **E**. My horses don't seem to mind that I only change the spread of **E** in this exercise.

Gymnastic exercise 5 (fold out pages 52 and 53)

This is a good exercise for horses who tend to 'rush' and for riders that have trouble maintaining their position. By 'rush' I mean that your horse is speeding up as he gets closer to the obstacle. Train your horse to keep a steady rhythm in the approach, because when the rhythm is under control, the balance is under control. Start with all of the rails removed from the standards except the first placing rail and the obstacle at **A**. Set **A** at 24ins (60cm). Jump several times at the trot, approaching the placing rail, taking two steps after the placing

Gymnastic exercises 3 and 4
Sequences

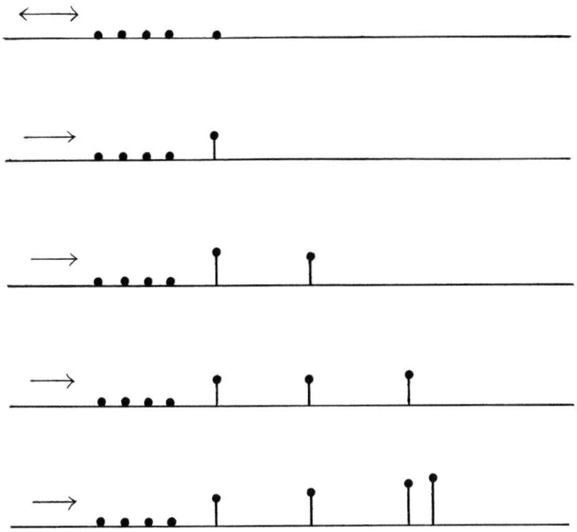

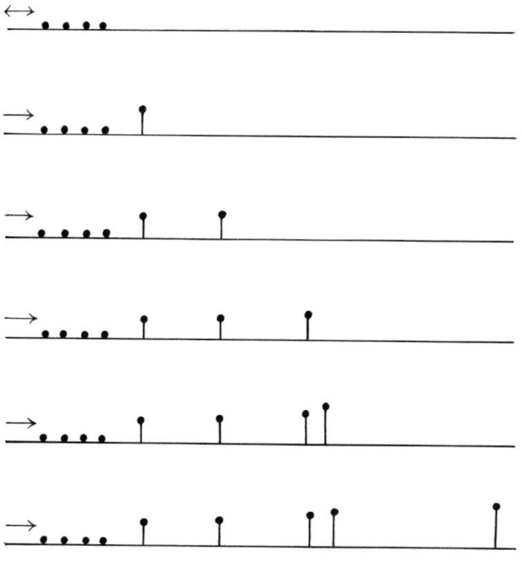

Gymnastic exercises 3 and 4: Distances

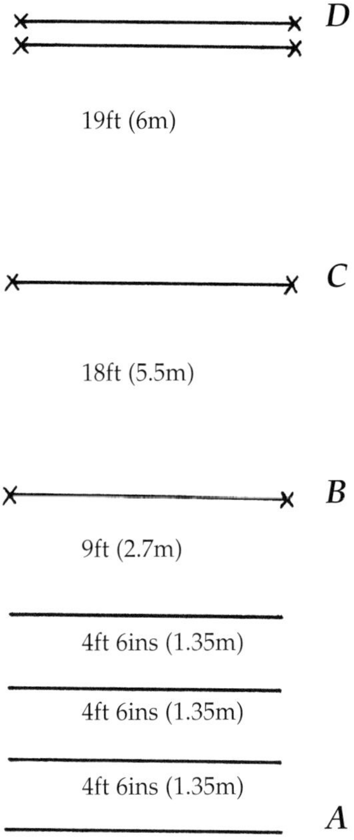

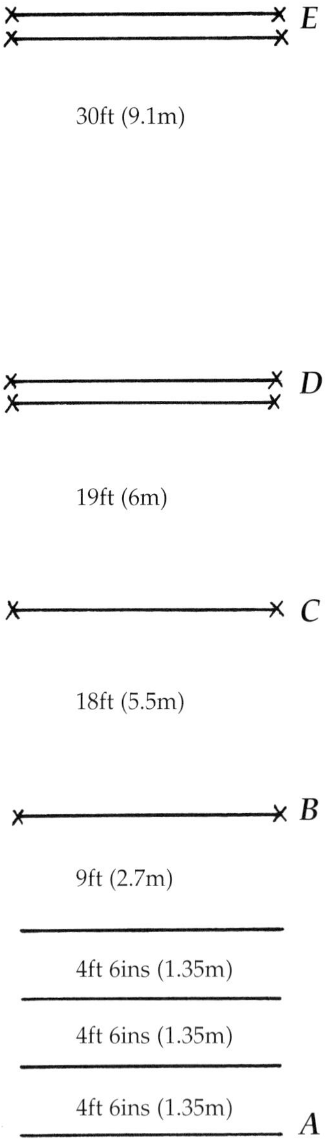

rail and jumping the obstacle at A, then reverse and work in the opposite direction.

This means that you will be approaching the obstacle through a line of open standards towards a vertical set at 2ft (60cm) high, with a 9ft (2.7m) placing pole on the ground behind the obstacle. Your horse should approach at the trot, jump the vertical, land at the canter, step over the 9ft (2.7m) placing pole without either attempting to put in a stride or attempting to land beyond the placing pole. This will teach your horse how to 'bounce' between obstacles.

Occasionally a horse will be startled by the placing pole on the ground behind the obstacle, and either refuse or over-jump badly. If he refuses, lower the obstacle until he will step over it and then raise it in small increments until he will jump the obstacle at its original height.

If he over-jumps and lands beyond the placing pole, move it out until your horse must land before the placing pole. You can then gradually move the pole back in to 9ft (2.7m). Make sure that you repeat this exercise until your horse understands it, as this is essential to teaching your horse to jump a bounce well, and to lower his head and neck in the air.

Once you and your horse are confident over this exercise in either direction, place a second obstacle in the standards at **B**. Trot back and forth several times both from the placing rail into the bounce and back from the bounce to the placing rail. Once your horse is calm and balanced you can add a rail at **C**. Repeat in both directions with a rail at **C** several times and then you can continue to **D**.

Approaching at the trot towards the placing pole before **A**, your horse will now double-bounce, take one stride at the canter, and jump **D**. When your horse jumps from **A** to **D** well, and trots calmly from **D** back to **A**, build **E**, **F** and **G** all at once, in order to cut down on the total number of repetitions.

When the entire exercise has been constructed your horse will approach the first placing pole at the trot, jump the first obstacle at **A** or **B**, bounce, bounce again, land, take one stride in the 20ft (6.1m) distance, jump the vertical at **D**, take a stride in the next 20ft (6.1m) distance, bounce, bounce again, and canter out over the last 9ft (2.7m) rail on the ground. Concentrate on maintaining your position throughout the exercise so that the horse's back can move freely underneath you. Remain poised in your two-point position during the bounce efforts and return to a light three-point position during the one-stride parts of the exercise.

If you are having trouble with your position in this exercise, use a neck strap to hold yourself in a two-point position. Concentrate especially on keeping a light, supple contact by relaxing your elbows and shoulders, and work on maintaining a straight line from your elbow to your horse's mouth. This double-bounce, one-stride, one-stride, double-bounce exercise causes the head and neck of your horse to move back and forth in a pronounced fashion. This will help you to learn how to maintain a consistent contact throughout the five phases of your horse's jumping effort.

One final comment about this exercise: the motion of your horse's head and neck when it jumps is not forward and back. The motions of your horse's head and neck when he jumps are ***back***, forward and back. In order to stay connected with the contact, remember that your elbow must come back towards your body as your horse coils onto his hocks and then stretches his neck forward into the jumping motion. This motion on your part must happen while your upper body remains still and poised above the horse's withers.

I mentioned earlier that this gymnastic is a good exercise to correct horses who rush. The most important part of this exercise is the double-bounce. This is because your horse can rush through a single bounce and land running, but he will find it very difficult to rush through double-bounces. Horses learn very quickly to keep their shoulders in front of them when going through these exercises, which teaches them to keep their balance.

As a variation to this exercise, you can remove the rails at **C** and **E**. This will now produce a bounce, two strides to a vertical , two strides to a bounce sequence. Furthermore, if you remove the vertical at **D**, you will then have a bounce, three stride, bounce sequence.

Gymnastic exercise 6 (fold out pages 56 and 57)

Exercise 6 is an important step in the education of your horse because it is the first time that we ask him to display some flexibility in the

Gymnastic exercise 5
Sequence

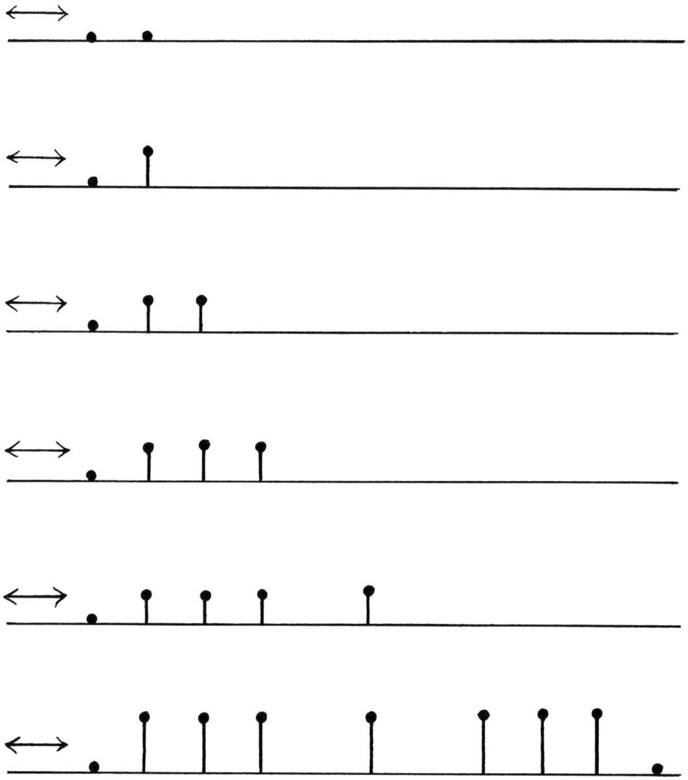

A variation

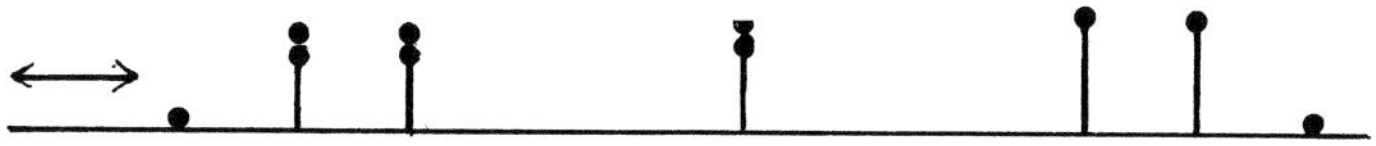

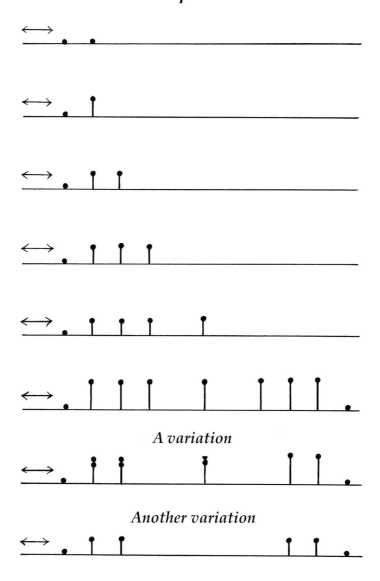

Another variation

Gymnastic exercise 5
Distances

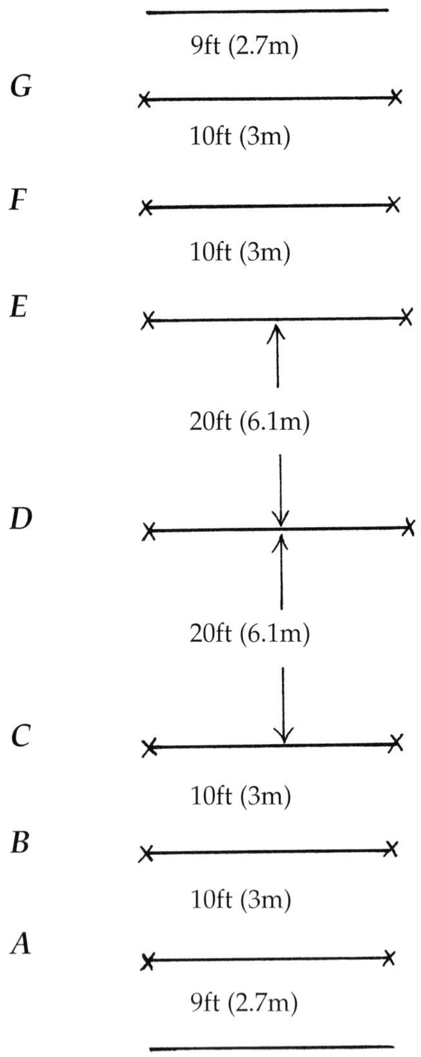

length of his stride. Proceed here as in exercise 2 (page 44). Trot your horse over the cavalletti both ways, then the obstacle at **B**, and then add **C**, proceeding from the cavalletti towards the obstacles.

The obstacles at **D** and **E** should be built before you start work. Build the oxers at **E** with a diagonal pole across the top of each oxer. Later in the lesson these oxers will get rather wide. I use the diagonal pole rested across the two oxer rails to help the horse realise that he needs to jump the whole thing (see Fig 8, below). There is always a possibility of the horse 'setting down' and putting his feet between the two rails of the oxer, especially when later you combine a low, wide oxer with bounces. This is of concern and we can prevent the horse from thinking that the oxer has become a bounce by using an additional diagonal pole. After that, unless you have a knock down, your exercise is set.

After trotting several times through the cavalletti and obstacles at **B** and **C**, trot in both directions over **D** with the obstacles set at about 24ins (60cm) wide. The distance inside **D**, 16ft (4.9m), is a slightly short stride for a normal horse approaching at the trot. This part of the exercise will teach your horse to shorten his stride before he jumps.

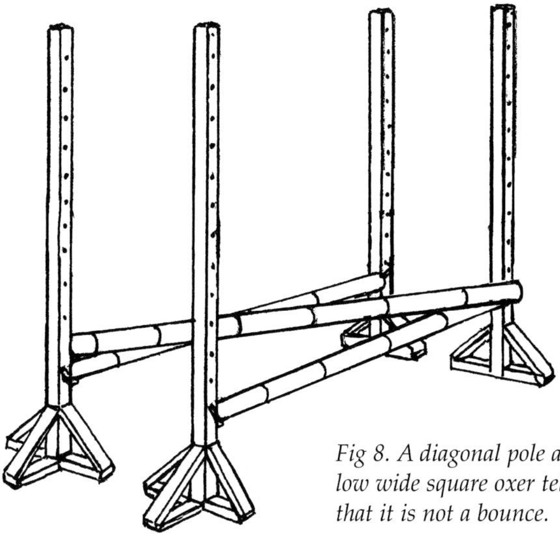

Fig 8. A diagonal pole across a low wide square oxer tells the horse that it is not a bounce.

When trotting towards **D**, imagine that there are four invisible rails on the ground set as cavalletti before **D**. This will help you maintain the regularity of the trot in the last two or three steps before the take-off. The horse should jump the first vertical at **D** normally. As your horse's front feet touch the ground you should land in a light three-point position, squeeze the reins without pulling back and use your voice, asking the horse to slow down. Your legs should remain in contact with your horse's sides, keep your heel soft. Remember to wait for your horse to take a full stride before jumping again.

Your sensation should be that of slow motion rather than that of increasing rapidity as you jump out of **D**. Repeat **D** several times in both directions until you are quite sure that your horse is adept at trotting over obstacles at least 3ft (90cm) high, 16ft (4.9m) apart, and producing one short stride each time. If your horse bounces out, instead of taking a short stride, put a pole on the ground halfway between the verticals.

Now proceed to the oxers set at **E** built with diagonal rails as illustrated on page 55. These should be no more than 18ins (45cm) high but 3ft (90cm) wide, set 32ft (9.7m) apart.

With very experienced horses, these oxers can be 2 ft (60cm) high and up to 6ft (1.8m) wide, still with diagonal rails across the top. Low, wide oxers produce a beneficial stretching of the top line and lowering of the head and neck, which will improve your horse's bascule. This gymnastic exercise produces quite a long two-strided result.

Approach **E** at a slightly strong trot with your reins very soft. The oxers are set purposefully quite low. Do not worry about knocking the oxer down but rather concentrate on getting across the distance in two strides. For example, as your horse leaves the ground at the first oxer at **E**, close your heels and think to yourself that you are riding across a ditch rather than jumping an oxer. As you land your action is the reverse of landing at **D**. Now you must close your heels, 'cluck' to your horse, make sure that your rein contact is soft, and urge your horse forward in two strides, jumping across **E**'s second oxer.

From the trot, 32ft (9.7m) is quite a long distance and I find that many horses will tend to 'chip in' a third stride during the first couple of attempts. You may support your leg with your whip at the point

Gymnastic exercise 6
Sequence

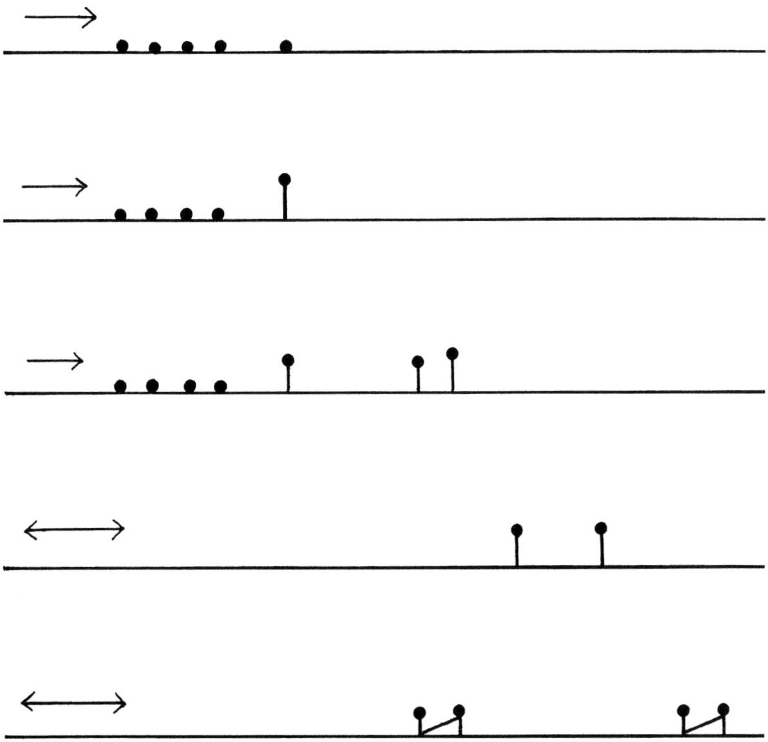

Gymnastic exercise 6
Distances

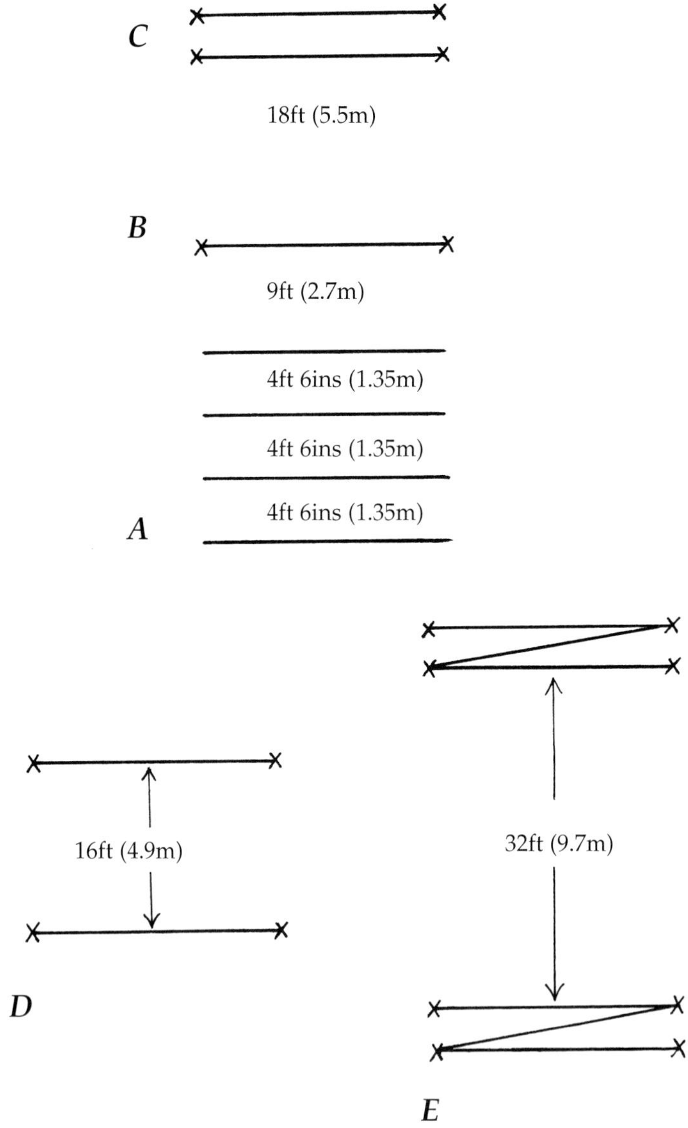

of take-off in front of the first oxer if necessary. If this correction is successful you should then repeat this exercise at **E** several times from both directions.

Practise this element until your horse gives you the sensation that he is starting to anticipate and moving forward of his own accord. No one can tell you how many times you will have to repeat this exercise until your horse understands it. My observation is that a very hot, quick-moving Thoroughbred will understand this exercise almost instantly. On the other hand, sluggish cold-blooded horses may need quite a bit of exposure to this exercise before they finally understand the concept. You should notice that between the oxer elements and the vertical elements, one of them will feel easy, and one will feel uncomfortable. This will tell you whether you need to emphasise lengthening or shortening your stride more.

Once you know this, you can start to design exercises which will help you deal with your own horse's particular problems. For example, if you have a horse who rushes, you should work from **A**, **B** and **C**, and then turn back to **B,** rather than allowing your horse to accelerate through the long distance at **E**. A horse who rushes and anticipates a long distance should be allowed to practise long distances occasionally, but should not be continually exposed to that particular problem. On the other hand, if your horse is sticky, you should emphasise **A**, **B** and **C**, and then **E**. Riders have a tendency to deal with exercises that they and their horses feel comfortable with. Instead, they should emphasise the exercise their horse finds more difficult. Practise jumping on a steady stride, a short stride or a long stride until you feel comfortable with any variation in your horse's stride.

So far, so good

This series of gymnastics does not necessarily have to be done from exercise 1 to exercise 6, but there is a logic involved in their development. This logic will help you educate your horse. If you do the exercises in the order they are presented, at least the first time the horse is introduced to them, you will make more rapid progress. Following this, you should not be afraid to go back from time to time and repeat some of the exercises.

Once you feel that your horse handles these gymnastics easily, you can increase their difficulty by increasing the height and the spread of the obstacles involved without altering the distances. Throughout the gymnastic training of the horse your chief goal is to ensure that your horse remains calm and balanced. If you can do this, you are well on your way to maximising your horse's full potential.

5

Advanced Jumping

Once your horse has done all of the exercises in Chapter 4, he is ready for more complex exercises. These will help you and your horse continue to develop your flexibility, control and skill. Hundreds of books have been written about what constitutes well-trained horses and how to train them to that level. I have read some of them, and the bibliography on page 130 will give you a list of some good books to read, if you want to continue your studies. However, having a well-trained horse comes down to this: if you can soften your hands, close your legs, and your horse surges forward, that is a good sign. When you soften your legs and squeeze your hands and your horse slows down, that is also a good sign. If you press with one leg against your horse's body, and he steps away from the pressure, that is also a good sign. If you soften one hand and squeeze the other, and your horse turns toward the firmer hand, that is a very good sign. When your horse does all of these things calmly and consistently, and can jump obstacles that are suitable in size and type for you and your horse without him losing his mental or physical balance, then he is well trained.

Gymnastic exercise 7 (fold out pages 62 and 63)

In exercise 7, you are now going to combine the skills that you practised in exercise 6, but in one connected series of obstacles, rather than as a single short exercise or a single long exercise as previously.

To begin work in exercise 7, take away all of the rails until you have your usual five warm-up rails on the ground. (The fifth rail will become the first obstacle when you raise it.) After your horse is calm and relaxed through this exercise put up your usual warm-up fence at **B**. Once your horse is settled in over this obstacle raise **B** in 6ins (15cm) increments until you have raised the rail at least a total of 1ft (30cm). If your horse is competing in show jumping or eventing, you should raise **B** until it reaches the height of your competitive level.

When your horse has jumped this obstacle to your satisfaction, walk and let him relax. Set the rail at **B** back to 2ft (60cm) and add a rail at **C** starting at 2ft (60cm) and raising it to 3ft 6ins (1.06m), increasing it in 6ins (15cm) increments. After several repetitions at 3ft 6ins (1.06m) give your horse another period of rest.

Put the rail at **C** down to a lower height and build the low, wide oxer at **D**. Remember to put a diagonal rail across this oxer and set it 18ins (45cm) in height but with a minimum of 3ft (90cm) in spread. Now trot through the cavalletti, jump the obstacle at **B**, take one long canter stride and jump **C** (this part of the gymnastic is similar to the work that you did in earlier exercises). When you land over **C** soften your reins, close your legs and lengthen your horse's stride. The aids that you use between **C** and **D** are the same aids that you used in exercise 6, jumping **E** (page 58).

If your horse responds correctly you should take one stride in this 20ft (6.1m) distance. Practise this gymnastic from the cavalletti to **B**, **C** and **D** several times, making the spread of the oxer 6ins (15cm) greater each time. You should be able to jump an 18ins (45cm) oxer with a 5–6ft (1.5–1.8m) spread quite easily. Remember to change the spread of the oxer by adjusting the back rail and not the front, as you do not want to alter the distance between **C** and **D** when you change the width of the oxer.

After a period of rest, return the spread of the oxer at **D** back to 4ft (1.2m). Add a rail in the standards at **E**, set about 2ft 6ins (75cm) high. Make sure that the distance from the back of the oxer at **D**, as it is now set, is 19ft (5.8m). Each time you change the back rail of the oxer you should adjust the distance to **E** to maintain the same distance, that is 19ft (5.8m). Your ground person is going to get quite a workout during this exercise.

You are now in a situation where you will trot in over the cavalletti, jump **B**, land and take a normal stride. Jump **C**, land and go forward

Gymnastic exercise 7
Sequence

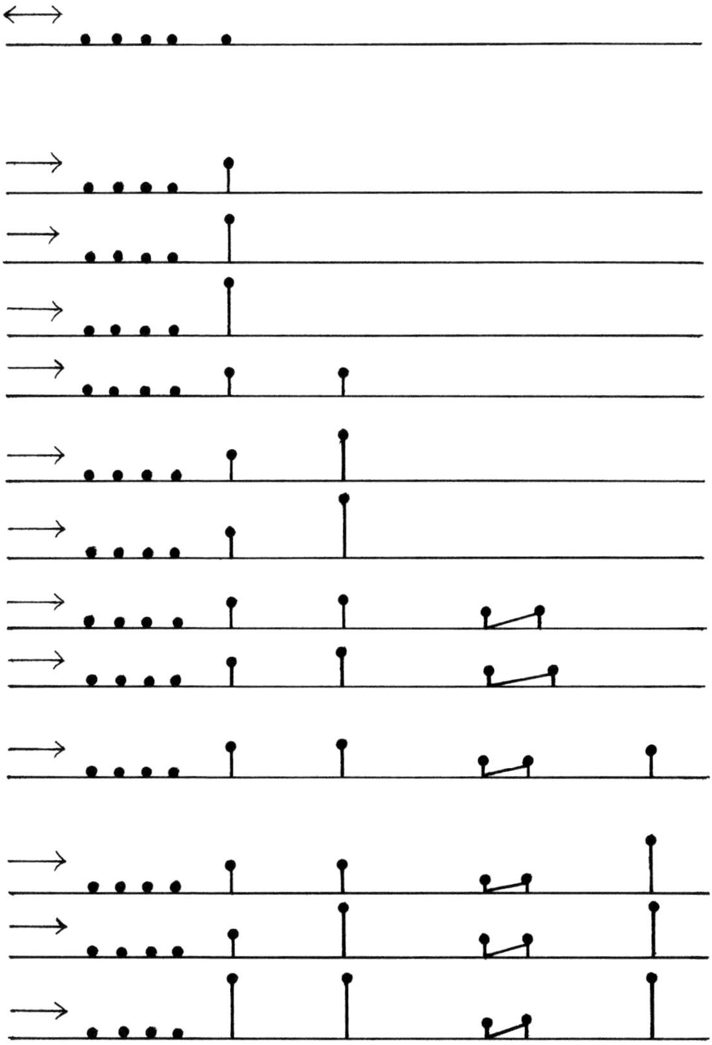

Gymnastic exercise 7
Distances

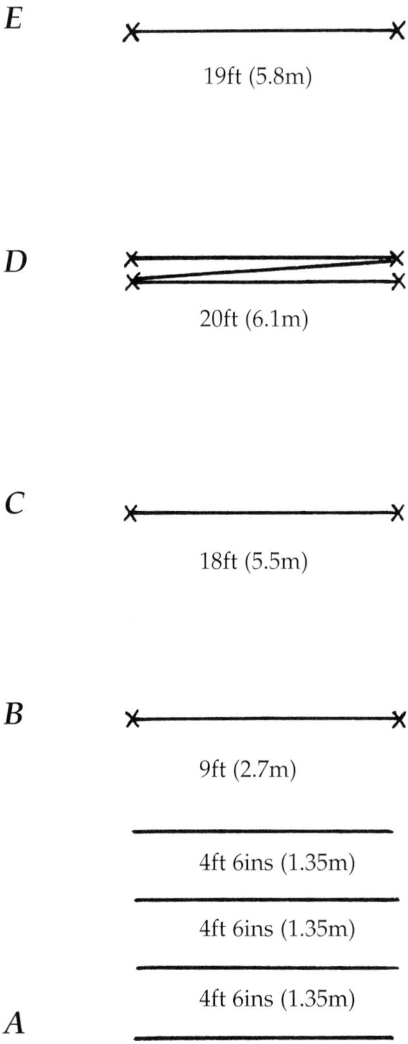

in your stride to **D**. Then you must land and shorten your horse's stride to jump **E** correctly. The aids used between **D** and **E** are the same aids that you used in exercise 6 at **D** (page 56), where you shortened your horse's stride between two vertical elements. Exercise 7 is more difficult than exercise 6, but it is not impossible for the normal horse. Your horse should know how to expand his stride and jump a wide fence from a long distance and then immediately return to balance and compress his stride in order to jump another obstacle from a shorter distance.

After your horse has satisfactorily jumped this exercise you can raise **E**, again in 6ins (15cm) increments, until your horse can jump from 3ft 6ins–4 ft (1.06m–1.2m) at **E**. After one or two repetitions of this entire exercise, a horse jumping in 3ft 6ins (1.06m) classes or eventing at 3ft 6ins (1.06m) should be able to come through this exercise with the obstacles set at 3ft (90cm) at **B**, 3ft 6ins (1.06m) at **C**, 2ft (60cm) high by 5ft (1.5m) wide at **D**, and 3ft 6ins (1.06m) at **E**. However, the first time you do this I would not be quite so enthusiastic with the height and spread.

Gymnastic exercise 8 (fold out page 68)

Exercise 8 is your first introduction to changing direction in a gymnastic situation. To construct this exercise, place a rail on the ground and build a vertical fence 9ft (2.7m) behind that, followed by a second vertical 18ft (5.5m) away as shown. On the plan, these are obstacles **A** and **B**. From obstacle **B** measure on a straight line 50ft (15.2m) and construct an oxer as shown at **E**. Put the rails for **E** on the ground at the side so that you can ride through the open standards at **E.**

Build **C** and **D** so that the left standard of **C** and the right standard of **D** are on the straight lines formed by the left and right standards of **B** and **E**.

The relationship of the obstacles at **C** and **D** is critical to your success with this exercise, so be very precise in your measurements. As always, use a measuring tape. Measure 36ft (11m) from the right end of the pole at **B** to the right end of the pole at **C**. Turn the pole at **C** until its left standard is on the straight line between the right standards of **B** and **E**. Set the height at about 2ft (60cm) to start.

Repeat this process to build the obstacle at **D**, measuring 24ft (7.3m) from the left end of the pole at **B** to the left end of the pole at **D**. Set the height as at **C**. Do not measure from the ends of the wings, as their widths may vary from one to another.

Warm up as usual and then begin work at the trot, with a placing pole 9ft (2.7m) from **A** on the ground. Then build a small warm-up jump at **A** and jump this several times. Follow this by building the obstacle at **B** and jump **A** to **B** several times. When you are satisfied that your horse is warmed up and prepared you may now jump from **A** to **B** to **C**.

The rider must be able to select which lead his horse will land on, which is a terrific advantage when doing a course. To practise this, use the following technique: as your horse takes off at **B**, open your right rein, and move your left rein over to the right so that it exerts a slight pressure against your horse's neck. Squeeze with your left leg and shift your weight over your right knee. Turn your head and eyes and look to the centre of the vertical at **C**.

This distance should produce three strides on a mild curve. Jump **A** to **B** to **C** several times until your horse understands the turn. If your horse misunderstands and runs out, he will usually refuse by sliding down the fence line to the left. Take one of the rails on the ground by **E** and construct a wing on the left side of **C**, and then continue with your training. Remove the wing at **C** later, to make sure your horse is responding correctly to your turning aids.

You should now attempt the turn to the left. Jump **A** to **B** to **D**, reversing the aids you used to turn to the right, that is, now open the left rein, use your right rein against the neck and close your right leg to press your horse into a curve to the left. Done correctly this exercise should produce two strides from **B** to **D**. Again, your horse may duck out – now to the right. This is understandable, as we have just spent five minutes or so teaching him to jump to the right going from **B** to **C**.

Do not become flustered if your horse runs out to the right at **D**. Take one of the rails from the ground at **E** and make a wing from the right hand standard of **D**. Repeat the left hand turning exercise several times. Your horse will quickly come to understand that he should listen to your aids in order to determine which direction he is going to go next. When you are successful, remember to remove the wing, to test if your horse now understands both turning aids.

Once horses understand this exercise, they become very adept at changing their direction. With practise, you will find that all you have to do to change direction is to open one rein and look – turn your head and eyes in the new direction – and your horse will seek that fence to the right or the left according to your actions.

While you give your horse a break, build an oxer at **E**. This oxer should not be too big; 3ft (90cm) in front and 3ft 3ins (1m) behind, with a 3ft (90cm) spread, should be sufficient to start. Now then, trot into the exercise and jump **A** and **B**, then take four slightly steady strides to **E**. The action of your reins on landing after **B** is the same as the actions you used to handle the short distance between the verticals at **D** in exercise 6 (page 56).

Land in a light three-point position with your hands at your horse's withers and squeeze the reins without pulling back. Do not sit down, or lean back and grip, as this will cause your horse to run through this exercise in three long strides rather than taking the desired four quiet, steady strides between **B** and **E**. Your horse will try to show off what he has learned and wander from **C** to **D**. This is normal and you should repeat **A** to **B** to **E** until he goes straight through. If your horse is 'hot', two or three repetitions is all you will need.

Once you have rehearsed all three possible lines through the gymnastic, you can start to do various courses. For example, trot in, jump **A**, **B**, **C**, and then continue left to canter over **D** in the opposite direction than you have been jumping it from the trot. You should have ground lines on both sides of **C** and **D** to facilitate this. Return to the trot and continue **A**, **B**, **D**, maintain the right canter lead and jump **C** in the other direction.

Return to the trot. Trot in, jump **A**, **B**, **E**, and quietly pull up to a halt. This pattern now allows you a great deal of variety in your direction and in your control over your horse's stride.

If your horse has trouble turning to the left, you should emphasise that curve from **B** to **D** If he has trouble to the right, emphasise that curve. Occasionally, if your horse is excitable, you can jump **A** and **B** and halt without jumping **C**, **D**, or **E**, reassure your horse and walk away from the exercise. In general, I do not like pulling event horses or racehorses up in front of obstacles, but I am willing to do it with any type of horse if he is extremely difficult and agitated in the approach.

Gymnastic exercise 9 (fold out page 69)

Exercise 9 is a continuation of training your horse to jump on curves. It will teach him how to be flexible in his length of stride. I call this exercise the 'cartwheel' for obvious reasons. Set the exercise up as shown with the verticals at about 2ft (60cm). After warming your horse up, trot and canter back and forth over **A**. Then trot and canter your horse back and forth over **B** and over **C** as individual obstacles.

Now, on a circle at a quiet canter, jump from **A** to **B** to **C** and continue **A** to **B** to **C**, and so on, remaining on the circle for up to six complete revolutions.

In the air over each obstacle use the same aids to turn as you did in exercise 8 (page 66). Open your inside rein, put your outside hand slightly against the withers, place your weight slightly over your inside knee and ankle, and look at the centre of the next jump.

A normal horse should produce five to six strides from **A** to **B**, three strides from **B** to **C**, and five to six strides from **C** to **A**. Your horse should be able to do three or four revolutions around the exercise in both directions without losing his rhythm.

As you work your horse in both directions around the cartwheel, be sure to note which direction causes your horse more trouble. This is invaluable information for you in the continuing education and improvement of your horse; for example, if he 'pops' his shoulder to the right, you know that you should emphasise right leg yielding and right shoulder-in.

Gymnastic exercise 10 (fold out pages 71 and 72)

This is a good exercise to teach your horse to keep his balance and to jump on a compressed stride. Begin the exercise with two rails on the ground 9ft (2.7m) apart at **A**. Trot back and forth through this several times until, as usual, your horse is calm, relaxed and balanced. Then raise the rail at **A** as shown and trot through this several times, stepping over the 9ft (2.7m) placing pole, taking two steps, jumping, and

Gymnastic exercise 8
Distances

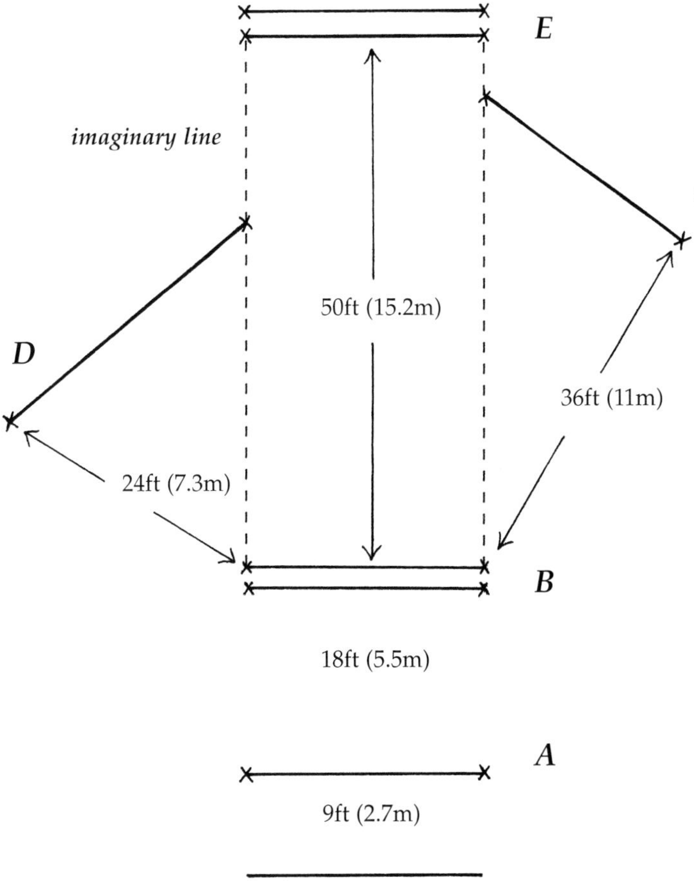

Gymnastic exercise 9
Distances

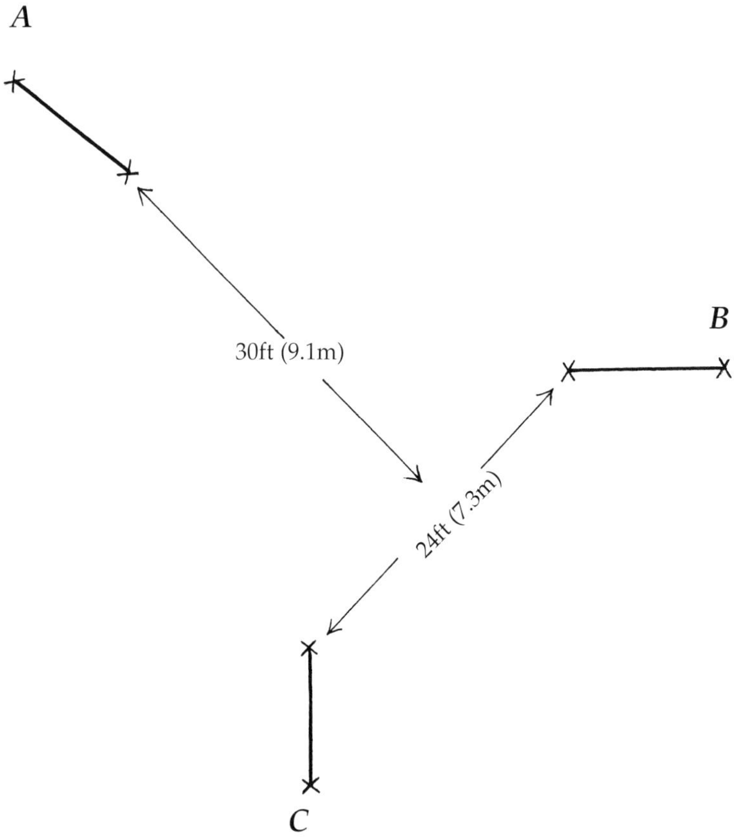

Gymnastic exercise 10
Distances

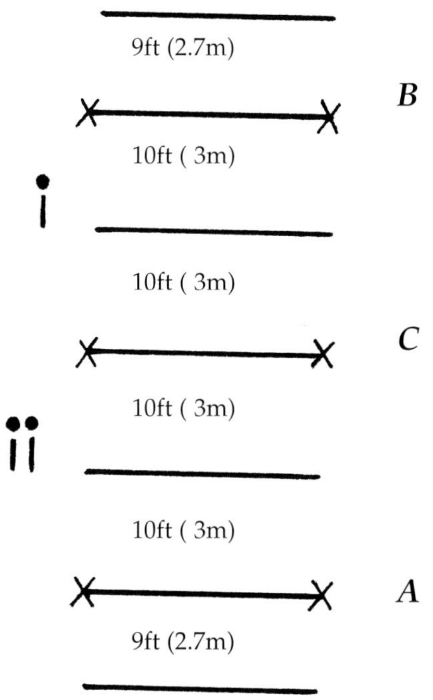

Gymnastic exercise 10
Sequence

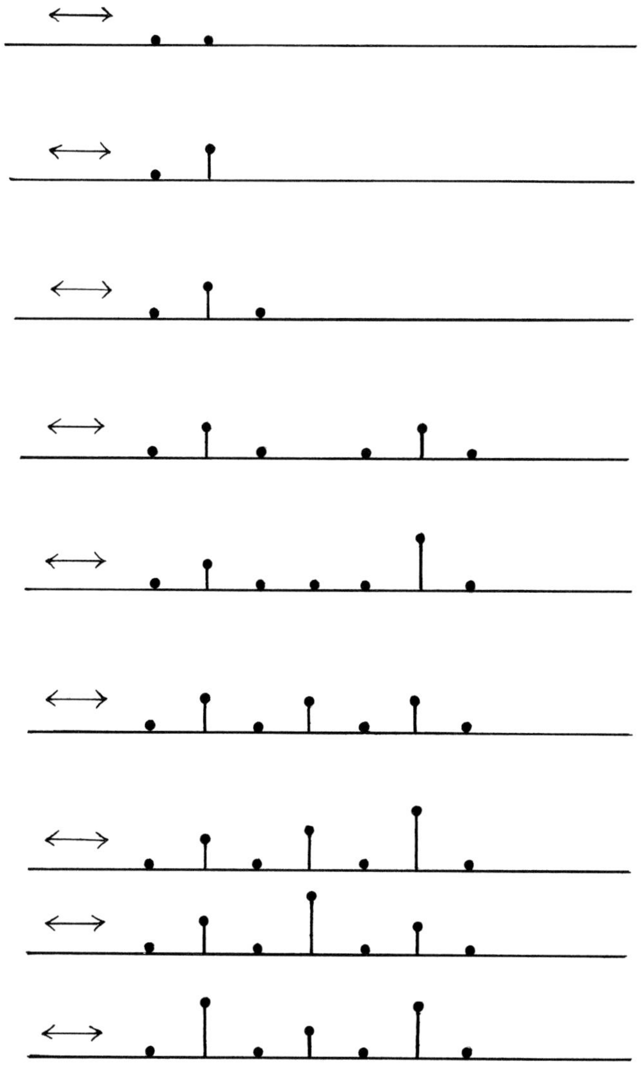

Gymnastic exercise 11
Distances

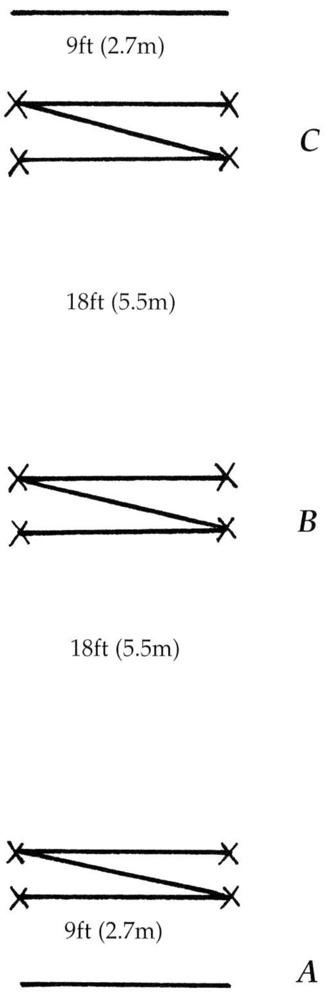

landing at the canter after the small vertical. After a few repetitions in this direction trot back the other way so that you are jumping the vertical first and landing, then cantering out over the placing pole.

Once your horse has accepted this and is obviously ready for further work, place another vertical at **B** as shown with a 9ft (2.7m) placing pole behind. Put placing poles down 10ft (3m) from the obstacles marked **i** and **ii** on the plan. You can now trot in, land, take three canter strides, and jump out over **B**. The rails on the ground will help maintain the regularity of your horse's stride.

You can practise going from **A** to **B** in three strides; then you can turn around and come back from **B** to **A**, having raised the fence at **A** until it is 6ins (15cm) higher than the fence at **B**. Quite often I will use this exercise to raise a horse's sights a bit and get them jumping a bigger fence than they might otherwise see in their daily course of business.

After having successfully come back and forth from **A** to **B** and **B** to **A**, lower fences **A** and **B** until they are approximately 2ft 6ins–3ft (75-90cm) high. Build the vertical at **C** as shown so that **A**, **C** and **B** are all the same height.

Now you can trot back and forth several times through this exercise. Starting from **A** you can raise **C** 3ins (7.5cm) and raise **B** 6ins (15cm), so that your horse has the sensation that he is jumping slightly uphill. You can vary the height of the three verticals, which is an excellent exercise to teach your horse to look at the height of the jump rather than jumping mechanically over rails of equal heights.

As your horse gains in balance and confidence, you should practise this exercise without the poles on the ground.

The number of repetitions and the height of the fences should be regulated so that your horse finishes his workout with enthusiasm and confidence.

Gymnastic exercise 11 (fold out pages 73 and 76)

Begin this exercise with two poles on the ground 9ft (2.7m) apart. Then, when your horse has settled in, build a vertical at **A** followed by an oxer also at **A**. **Whenever you see a diagonal line across an oxer in one of my sketches it means that I want you to make the spread**

wider than the height. For example, you could build this oxer 18ins (45cm) high but it should be 3ft (90cm) wide. I use fences of this shape to stretch a horse's top line, to lower his head and neck in the air over the obstacle, and to teach him to push more with his hindquarters.

Trot back and forth over these elements until you and the horse are warmed up, comfortable and confident.

Place another oxer of equal dimensions 18ft (5.5m) away from **A** and trot through several times. Trot over the placing pole, jump the first oxer, land and take one canter stride and jump the second oxer. It is good for you to come back the other way in trot, that is from **B** to **A,** because a little more accuracy in riding is required when you approach the low, wide oxer without a placing pole in the approach.

Again, you should practise this until your horse is relaxed and understands the questions that are being asked. Then you can add a further oxer at **C** with a 9ft (2.7m) placing pole behind it. Practise back and forth several times. If your oxers have been set at 18in (45cm) high by 3ft (90cm) wide throughout, even an inexperienced horse should find this exercise easy to do and, indeed, may start to rush a bit. If this is the case, it is time for you to start raising the oxers. I raise all of the oxers at once and, at least during the first introduction to this exercise, I keep the spread the same so that, at some point, the height of the oxer will become greater than the spread. Until I am sure that the horse understands the question being asked, I will be a bit conservative with the spread.

Later on, I increase the spread of the oxers as well as the height. Remember to maintain the same distance between the obstacles and placing poles. For example, if you move the spread at **A** you should move the front rail away from the exercise and adjust the placing pole accordingly. If you change the spread at **B** you should re-measure the entire exercise, as this will change the distances between the obstacles. Your helper on the ground will be able to skip their visit to the health club after this session.

You must be aware that this exercise quickly changes in nature from being quite easy to becoming quite difficult as the interplay of the height, spread and the 18ft (5.5m) distance becomes more complex. It is easy to overface a young horse by asking him to do too much in this

Gymnastic exercise 11
Sequence

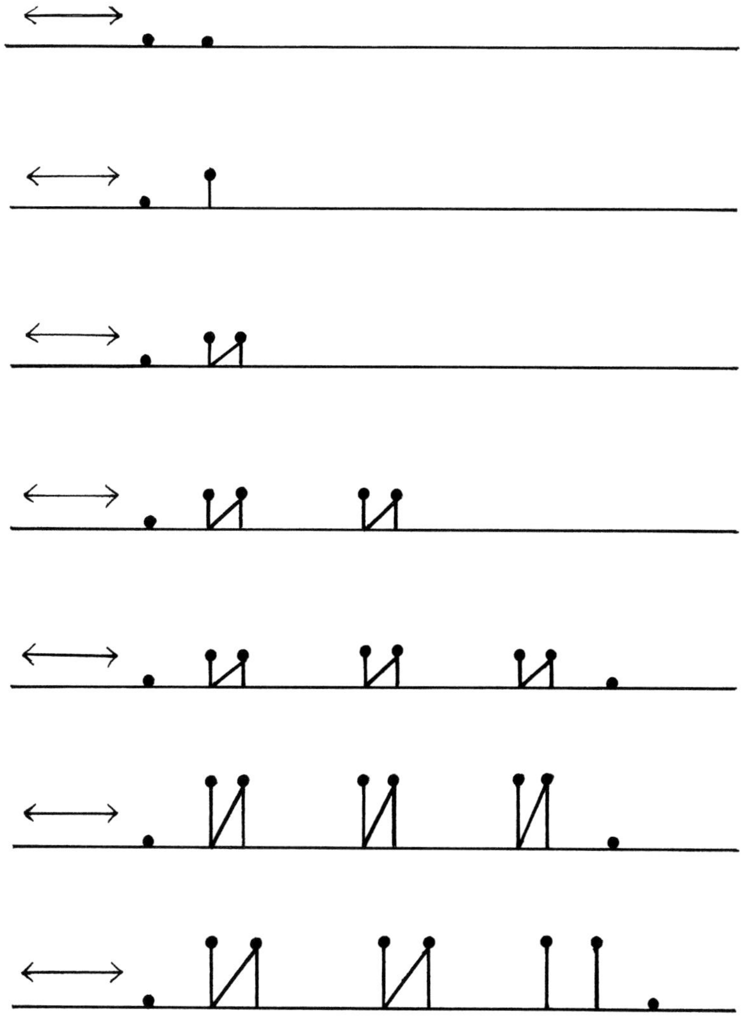

Gymnastic exercise 12 Distances

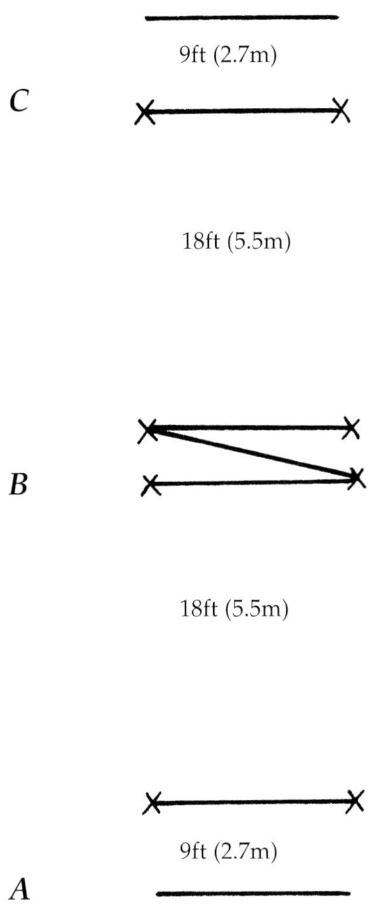

exercise. If you make a mistake, you should be conservative rather than aggressive in raising the heights and spreads.

Gymnastic exercise 12 (fold out pages 77 and 79)

Begin exercise 12 with two poles on the ground 9ft (2.7m) apart. Once your horse is comfortable here, build a vertical at **A** as shown and trot into this several times at the height suitable for your horse. Approach at the trot from both directions so that your horse is comfortable going either way.

Now build the oxer at **B**. Again, note the diagonal lines across the oxers in the sketch. This means that the spread is greater than the height and the oxers should be built to produce this result.

Trot back and forth from the vertical to the oxer, **A** to **B**, and then from the oxer at **B** in one stride back to **A**. When your horse is settled in, you can then add the vertical at **C** with a 9ft (2.7m) placing pole behind **C**, and the gymnastic is complete as shown on page 77.

Enter towards **A** at the trot, jump the vertical, take one stride, jump the low, wide oxer, take one stride, and finish over the vertical at **C**. You can increase the difficulty by raising the verticals at **A** and **C** while maintaining the low, wide oxer as it was originally set. Thus, your horse must compress his stride to jump the first vertical, stretch his body out over the low, wide oxer at **B**, and finally recover his balance in order to rock back on his haunches and jump the vertical at **C**.

At some point I move the last placing pole at **C** out to 10ft (3m), as the verticals get bigger. This relationship will change according to the horse and the height of the fence being jumped. The important points are that you want your horse to drop his head and neck over the vertical, and look where he is going to put his feet down behind the last fence.

There may be a slight tendency by your horse to rush between **B** and **C**. Make a concerted effort to stay poised over the horse's withers and jump the exercise on soft reins. Throughout the training of your horse it is essential that you teach him to stay in balance without depending on the contact with your reins. If the horse becomes more and more exuberant, you can place poles on the ground 9ft (2.7m) in front of and 9ft–10ft (2.7–3m) after the oxer at **B**. This will assist your horse in maintaining the regularity of his stride.

Gymnastic exercise 12
Sequence

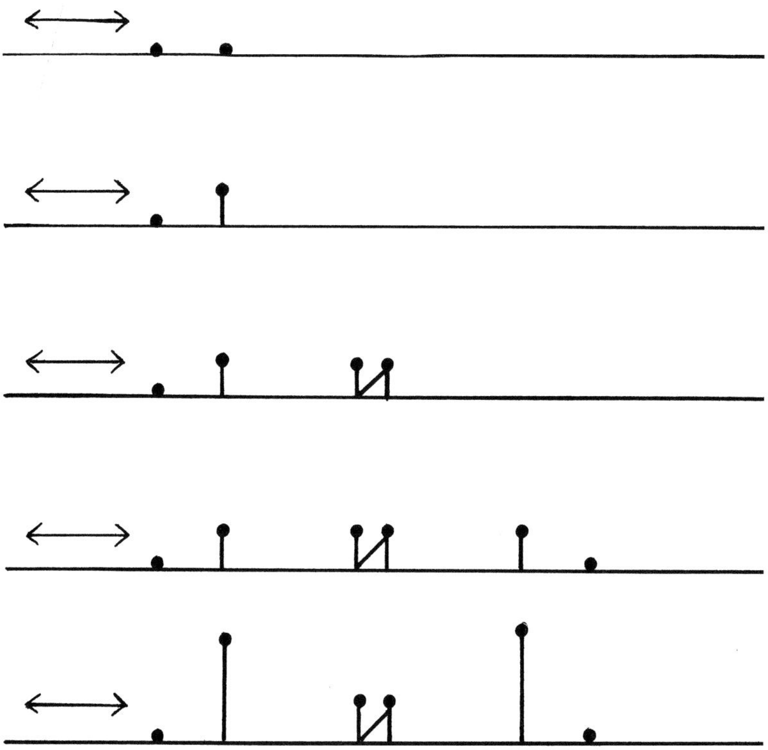

Gymnastic exercise 13
Distances

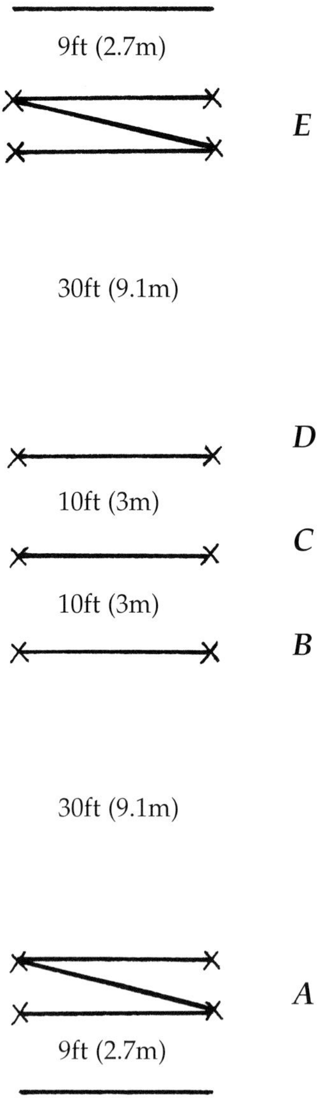

Gymnastic exercise 13 (fold out pages 80 and 82)

This exercise is the reverse of exercise 12. In the latter, we asked your horse to compress his body, then expand, and then compress his body again. In this new exercise , we are going to ask your horse to expand his body first, then compress during the double bounce, and then expand his body again out over the final low, wide oxer.

If you have enough rails and standards, it is a very good idea to have exercises 12 and 13 set up side by side. Then if your horse becomes overly exuberant during exercise 12, you have an alternative immediately at hand which will teach him to re-balance himself. The double bounce in the middle of exercise 13 has a wonderfully compressing effect on the length of your horse's stride.

Start as usual with the poles on the ground 9ft (2.7m) apart and then build a vertical at **A**. When your horse is comfortable jumping the vertical at the trot, turn fence **A** into a low, wide oxer. Trot several times back and forth until your horse is relaxed. Then, 30ft (9.1m) away, add a single bounce at **B** and **C**. Trot again back and forth several times until your horse understands the distance and the striding. For example, if you trot in over **A** your horse should land in canter, take two regular strides and jump the bounce at **B** and **C**. When your horse is comfortable going in either direction, you can add the second bounce at **D.** Again, trot both ways several times. The final oxer at **E** should be the same height and spread as the oxer at **A**. You can now approach the entire exercise at the trot from either direction.

The difficulty of this exercise can now be increased in two ways. First of all, you can raise the verticals at **B**, **C** and **D**, which will cause your horse to compress his body a great deal more. Once he is comfortable with this change in his environment, you can then spread the oxers at **A** and **E**. Remember to move the outside rail to change the spread, and to re-measure the 9ft (2.7m) distance to the placing pole in both directions. By the time you have done all of the repetitions which lead up to the complete exercise, you should only go through the whole exercise a maximum of twice each way. That will be enough jumping for your horse, especially if it is the first time he has done this exercise.

Gymnastic exercise 13
Sequence

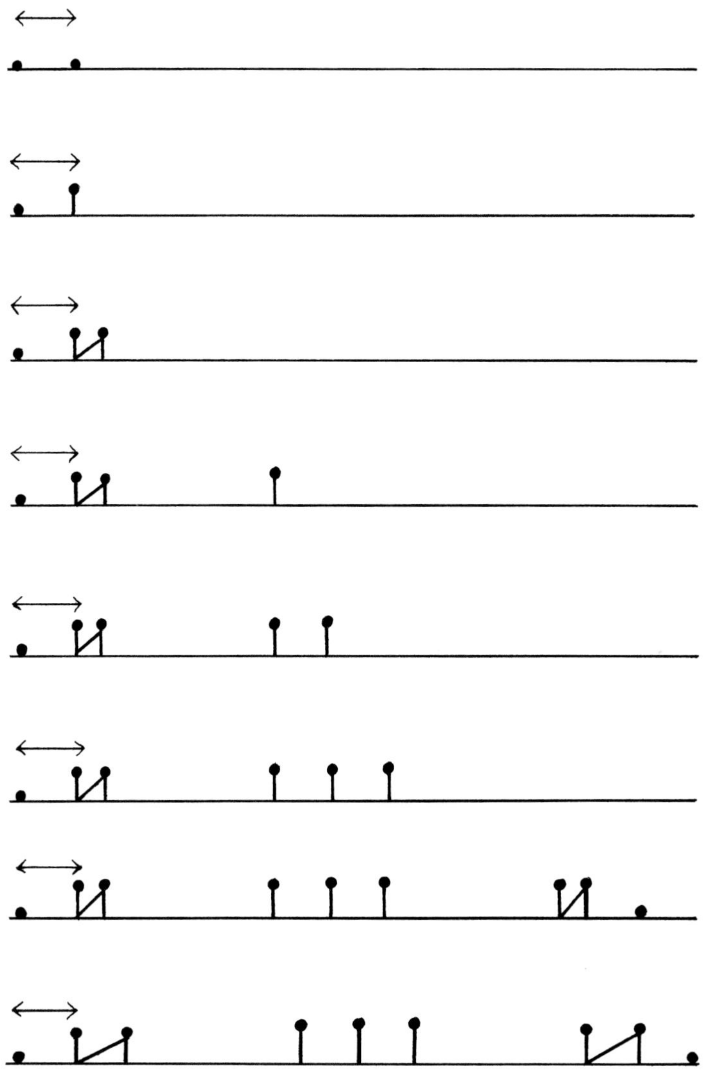

Gymnastic exercise 14 Distances

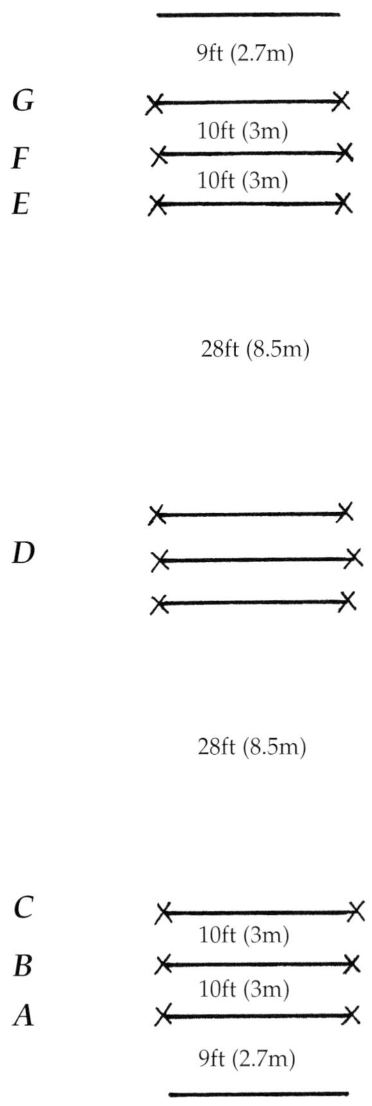

Gymnastic exercise 14 (fold out pages 83 and 85)
This is one of my favourite exercises to teach horses not to rush. Begin exercise 14 as usual with two poles on the ground 9ft (2.7m) apart. Build a small vertical and trot back and forth over these elements to warm your horse up.

At this stage of your horse's training he should be quite businesslike in his approach toward these exercises, and I think you can proceed to build the obstacles without too many repetitions. First of all,trot back and forth over a single bounce at **A** and **B** and then a double bounce, going out of trot, **A**, **B** and **C**. Then returning at the trot, bounce **C**, **B** and **A**. When your horse is relaxed in this exercise you can then build a hog's back at **D**, 28ft (8.5m) away from **C**. I like to keep the first and last rails of the hog's back quite low, raising only the middle rail to increase the difficulty of this fence. Trot a couple of times from **A** to **B** to **C**, land in canter and continue in two strides to the hog's back at **D**.

The distance is designed to place your horse's front feet quite close to the hog's back. At first this might be a slightly uncomfortable sensation for you and your horse, but you should get used to it, as this is the correct place to take-off in front of fences of this shape. When you are comfortable going through the double bounce, landing, taking two strides and jumping out over the hog's back, you should then approach the hog's back at **D** at the canter, jump it, land and take two strides coming out in the other direction over the double bounce. At this point you can go ahead and build the second set of bounce rails at **E**, **F** and **G** because, in effect, the horse has already seen this part of the exercise when you came back at the canter from **D** towards **C**, **B** and **A**.

The horse can now trot in both directions over this exercise. Gradually you should raise the middle rail of the hog's back until the horse is jumping what is, for him, quite a large obstacle.

Younger horses seem to understand this exercise well enough but I usually move the outside rails of the hog's back closer to the centre element, thus increasing the distance slightly between the hog's back and the bounces and also decreasing the spread of the hog's back. Once your horse has seen this exercise a couple of times, he should be

Gymnastic exercise 14
Sequence

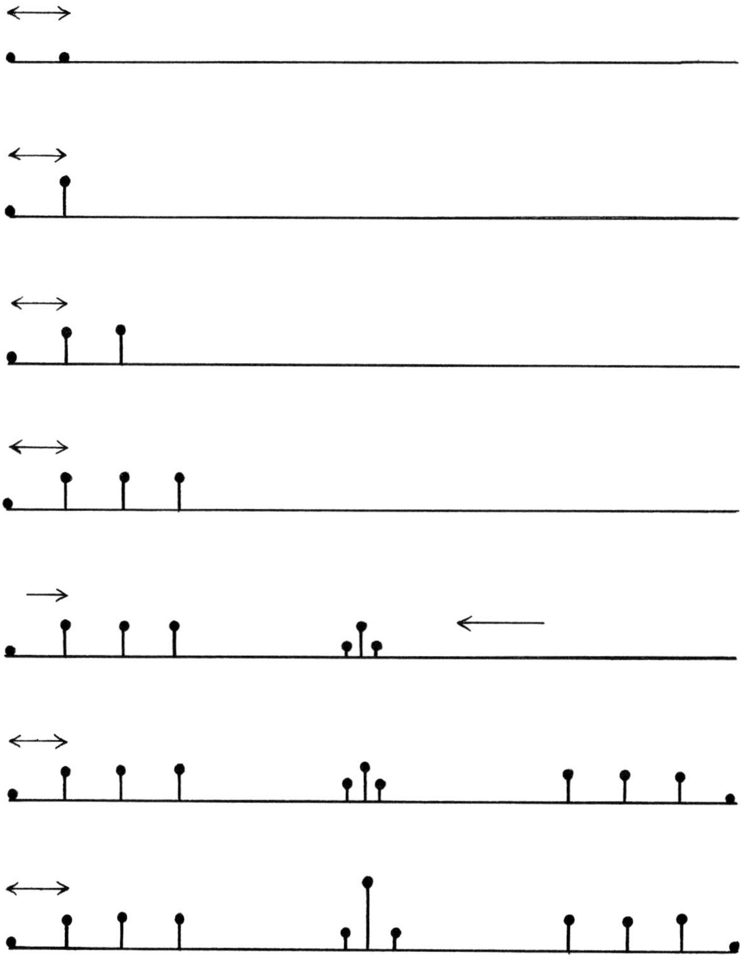

able to jump a hog's back with a spread of 5ft (1.5m) and a height at the centre rail of 3ft 6ins (1.06m) quite easily.

If your horse becomes a bit exuberant after jumping a larger hog's back, you can start to raise the double bounce rails at **A**, **B**, **C** and **E**, **F**, **G** as a deterrent. Just as in the last set of exercises, try to teach your horse to keep his own balance rather than pulling back on the reins. Horses can rush through a single bounce and jump that sort of exercise 'over their shoulders' (on their forehand). However, they will very quickly learn not to over-commit themselves when jumping a double bounce because they have to keep their centre of balance behind their shoulder in order to negotiate the exercise safely.

Cross-Country Gymnastics

Cross-country gymnastics have the same benefit to your horse as regular show jumping gymnastics and should be done with the same ideas in mind. Your horse should maintain his balance and regularity, and you should be poised over the centre of gravity, riding with soft reins throughout these exercises. Even if your horse is going to be a show jumper, some work up and down slopes can be very beneficial to him, as it teaches him to keep his balance going downhill and to push with his hocks going uphill, and balance and energy are what the jumping game is all about.

Gymnastic exercise 15 (see pages 88 and 89)

Begin your cross-country gymnastic work on a very mild slope. Put two poles on the ground 9ft (2.7m) apart, and then trot uphill and downhill over them. Be aware of the influence of the terrain on you and your horse's balance. For example, when you are trotting uphill your weight must be even more determinedly in your heels, the inclination at your waist should be greater; and although soft and light in the contact, your reins should be slightly shorter as a reminder to keep your balance up over your horse's shoulders.

On the other hand, when trotting and later cantering downhill over the rails on the slope your reins should be a bit longer, your lower leg should be slightly in front of the girth and the angle at your hip should be a bit more open to assist you keeping your centre of gravity behind your horse's shoulders. Going either uphill or down, your stirrup leathers should remain vertical.

Once you feel comfortable trotting and cantering over the rails on

Gymnastic exercise 15
Distances

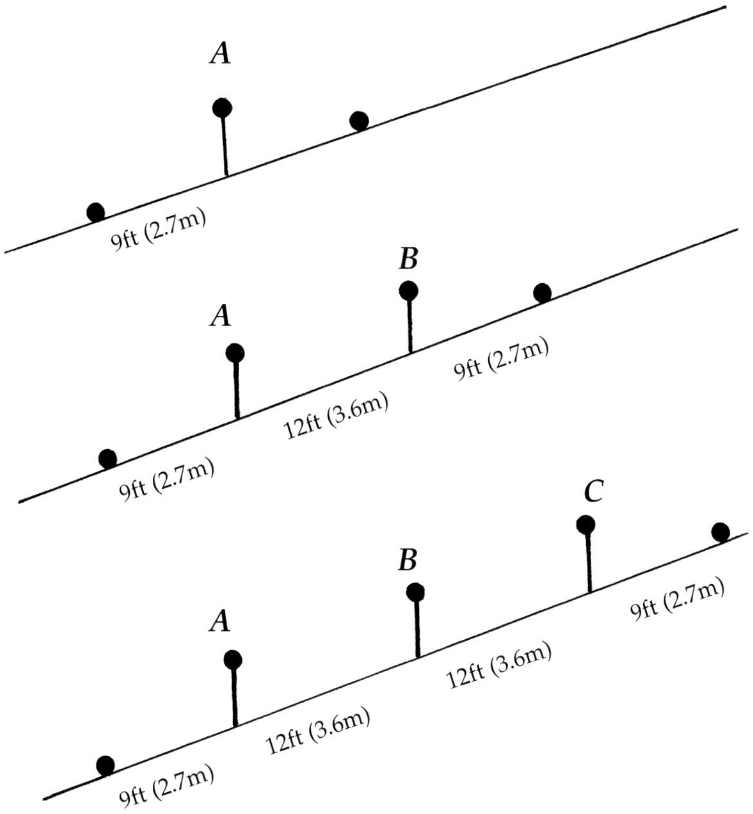

Gymnastic exercise 15
Sequence

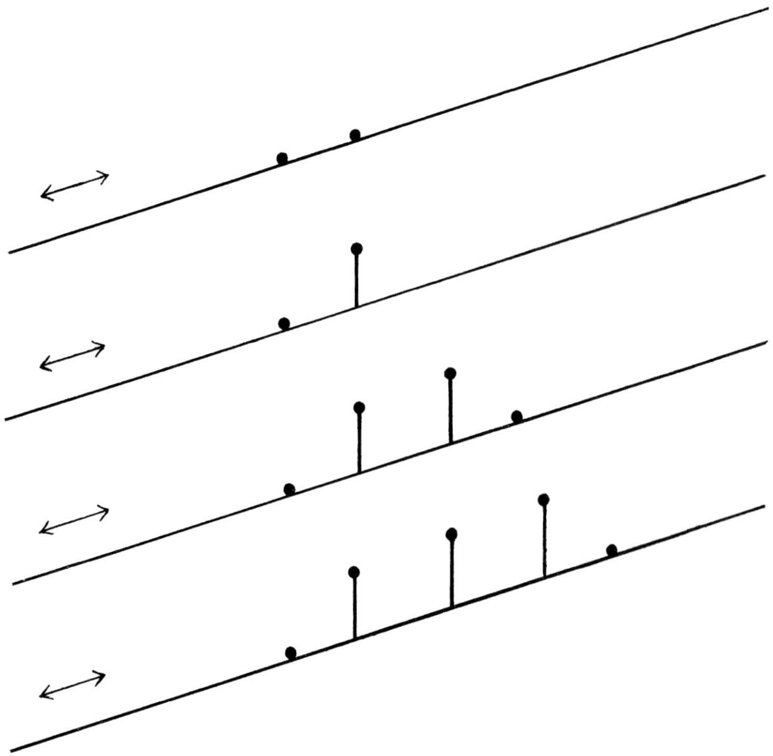

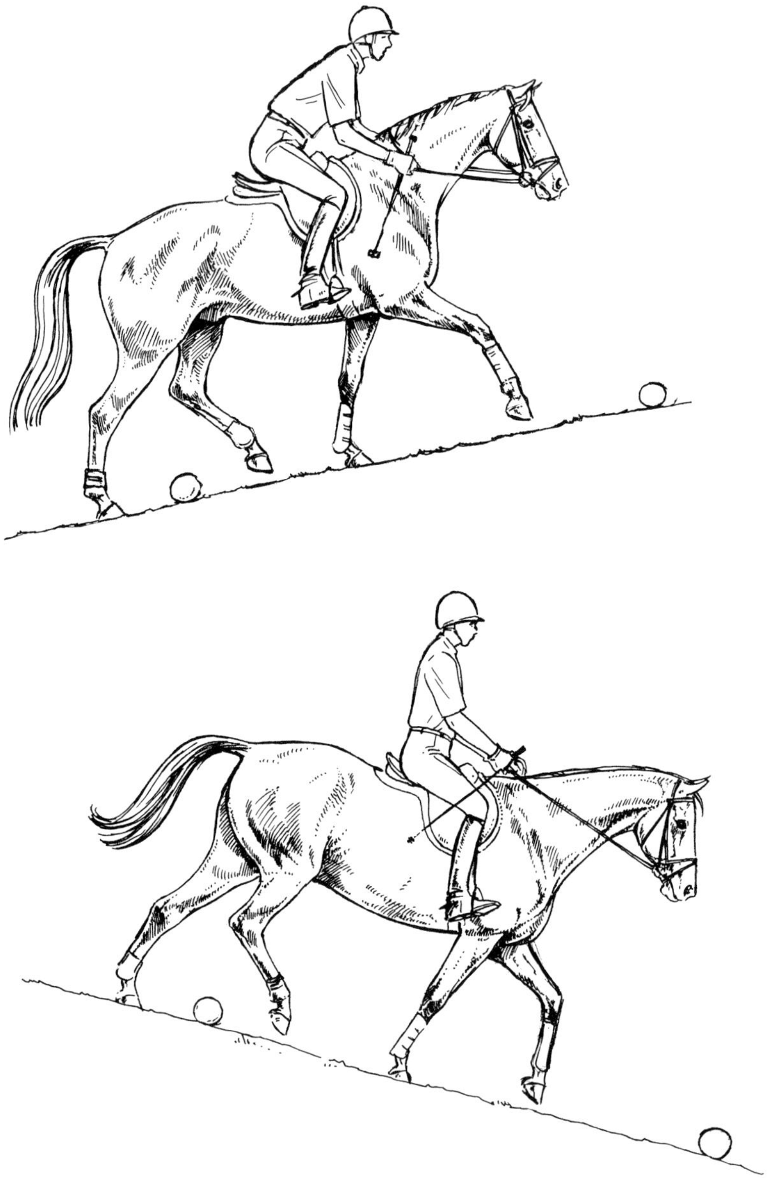

Fig 9a. A rider's position going up slopes (top); and Fig 9b, down slopes (above).

the ground, build an obstacle as shown in exercise 15 on page 88, with a 9ft (2.7m) placing pole before and after the fence. Practise back and forth over a small obstacle at both trot and canter until you are comfortable jumping up and jumping down. Remember that jumping uphill you should land after the vertical with the weight very much in your knees and ankles. It is easy for you to fall behind the motion jumping uphill, just as it is easy for you to topple in front of the motion jumping downhill. Both mistakes interfere with your horse's balance, so work hard to prevent them from happening.

If you are having trouble staying with the motion jumping uphill, you should move your lower leg farther behind the girth. This will make it easier for you to keep your shoulders up over your horse's withers when he lands going uphill. Alternatively, if you are toppling over your horse's neck and landing in a precarious position when your horse jumps downhill, you must move your lower leg forward until your stirrup leather is slightly in front of the vertical. This, coupled with slipping the reins slightly, will allow you to land in balance and safety.

When you are comfortable trotting and cantering up and downhill you can then place a second vertical 12ft (3.6m) away from the first, with a 9ft (2.7m) placing pole behind it. You should notice that I have used a 12ft (3.6m) distance in the bounce cross-country, while I used a 10ft (3m) distance in the bounces on flat terrain. This is because when your horse is jumping downhill he will need a little more room to land than on the flat, and when jumping uphill, the distance will be slightly long, which is a good thing as it encourages your horse to push his body forward and encourages you to ride with your lower legs not with your reins. In addition, you now have an exercise which can be jumped in both directions.

After you have practised over the single bounce at **A** and **B**, add a third rail at **C**, to create a double bounce.

Once your horse is comfortable trotting and cantering straight uphill and straight downhill over the double bounce you should vary your work by approaching on a curve. For example, canter on the left lead turning left-handed uphill up to the double bounce, jump the exercise, and pull up going up the slope. Then turn and come back downhill on the left lead practising turning across and down the slope into the double bounce exercise.

Your horse should be equally balanced on both leads in this and you should decrease the amount of time that the horse has to look at the exercise as you go along so that he becomes accustomed to meeting fences and thinking about them quickly while dealing with the problems posed by changing terrain.

Gymnastic exercise 16 (fold out pages 94 and 95)

For this exercise you will need a small permanent bank. In order to teach the horse about banks in the simplest possible manner, I prefer to begin with square banks, which are on level ground. The height of the bank should be approximately 2ft (60cm), and if possible I do not want a log at the top of it as I prefer to simulate a jump here with portable rails. This allows me to regulate the effort according to the reaction of the horse to the situation.

Trot and canter both ways up and down the bank. Review in your mind the comments regarding the placement of your body over the horse jumping uphill and downhill. The motion jumping up and down banks is merely an exaggerated form of the sensations you have already received when jumping up and down a slope during exercise 15.

Once your horse is comfortable trotting and cantering up and down the bank, place two rails on the ground 9ft (2.7m) apart on the top level of the bank, 18ft (5.5m) from the edge. Trot from the rails to the bank first so that your horse looks at the change to the exercise, and then steps down over a bank which he has already jumped. The standards that will be used for obstacles **A** and **B** should be in position, but without rails yet. This allows your horse to see where the standards are, and reminds you to proceed in a straight line both towards the obstacle and going away from the obstacle.

Trot and canter this exercise with the rails on the ground. When your horse understands the situation you can then place a vertical at **A** as shown. Trot from the 9ft (2.7m) placing pole to **A**, land, take one stride, and allow your horse to step down and canter out through the open standards at **B**. If the terrain is level, then when your horse jumps the obstacle at **A**, you should be in a normal show jumping position.

Fig 10a. 'Slipping' the reins when jumping down a drop.

When he lands and takes his stride before the bank, you should also remain in a normal show jumping position.

As your horse steps down off the bank the sensation you should have is that you push the points of your hips forward and down and soften your fingers so that your horse can stretch his head and neck down into the landing after the bank. Do not take an exaggerated position backward with your head and neck, as this will cause you to lift your hands up and back, thus pulling on your horse's mouth and interfering with the use of his head and neck.

As you canter away from the bank, lift your reins with one hand and slide them through the fingers of your other hand thus re-establishing a normal length. This will not come naturally to you at first and it is something that you should practise when you are walking around the field.

When you slip the reins to follow your horse's mouth down the

Gymnastic exercise 16
Distance

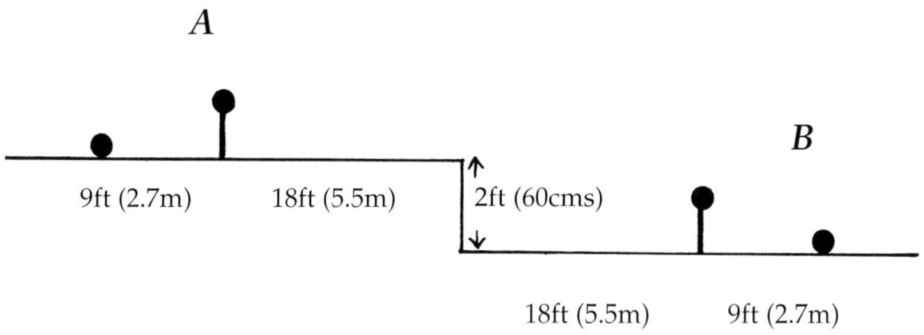

Gymnastic exercise 16
Sequence

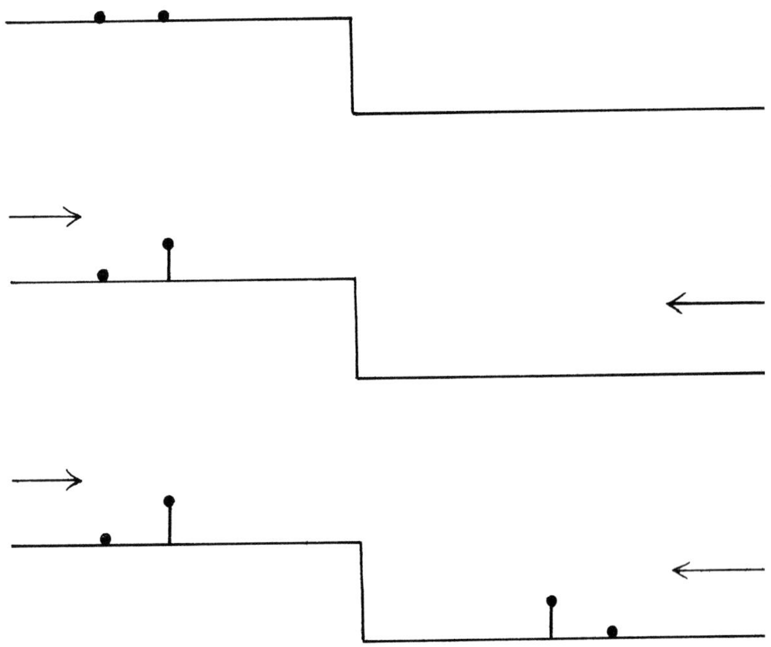

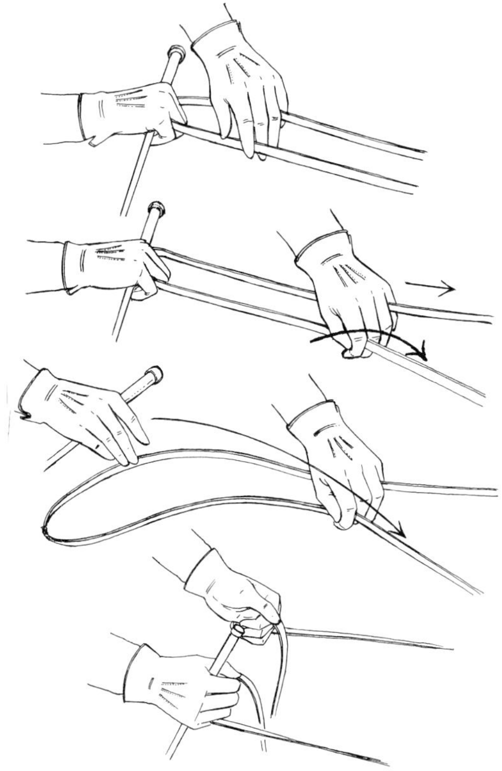

Fig 10b. A quick method of recovering the reins.

drop, re-establish the correct length of rein and contact as soon as you can (see Fig 10a, page 93, and above).

It is usually easier on your horse to trot at **A**, then jump down the bank. When jumping up the bank, approach at the canter, jump the bank, take one stride and jump the vertical at **A.** Once the horse is comfortable with this you can add the vertical at **B** and the 9ft (2.7m) placing rail as shown. Approach at the canter from **B** towards the bank so that the new part of the exercise is the first part that the horse sees.

I find that if you approach from the other direction, **A** to **B**, often the less experienced horse will make a mistake at **A** because he has lost his

Fig 11. Hollowing the horse's back is not desirable when jumping down a bank.

concentration due to looking ahead at the new element at **B**. Once your horse has jumped successfully, landing over **B**, taking a stride, jumping up the bank, taking another single stride, jumping again, and landing after **A** in a poised and balanced fashion, you are ready to come back the other way around.

This is a tricky moment because the sensation that you will have when jumping down the bank is that **B** is too close. Do not panic and pull back on the reins in an attempt to shorten your horse's stride. Like so many things in riding this actually creates the condition that you were trying to prevent. When you pull back on the reins you invert your horse's back. This will cause him to jump farther off the bank, thus landing too close to **B** and making an awkward effort or indeed knocking down the obstacle at **B** (see Fig 11).

Your actions should be thus: a pproach at the trot and jump **A**. Land with your reins organised. As your horse steps to the end of his stride before jumping down the bank, let the reins soften so that he can lower his head and neck. Your thinking should not be that you want to pull your horse's stride away from the take-off point before **B** *but rather* that you want him to step down quietly, close to the base of the bank after **A**.

Once you think about this, it becomes obvious that the closer we can land behind the bank the more room we will have to fit in our stride and the more comfortable our effort will be jumping out over **B**. If your horse is green and 'launches' off the bank, you can usually solve this problem by putting a placing pole 9ft (2.7m) between the bank and the vertical at **B**. Practise this exercise a great deal if you are a cross-country rider because it simulates so many of the situations that you will find yourself in when going across country.

Once your horse has become adept jumping from **A** to **B** and **B** to **A**, you can start to alter the distances. For example, you can move **A** in until it is 10ft (3m) from the lip of the bank which will cause the horse to land over **A**, bounce down the bank, take a stride to **B**. Alternatively, jumping back from **B** to **A**, your horse will jump **B**, take one stride, step up on the bank and bounce out over the rail at **A**.

I usually place rails on the ground first when I am doing these exercises to show the horse where the obstacle will be the next time through. It is very useful to make the obstacles small at first so as to make sure that your horse understands the exercise. Once he understands the questions asked, the height and spread will be no problem.

There are other exercises that we can set up using portable rails. For example, we can teach our horses to jump narrow fences, corners and bounces both before and after the bank. By changing the location of the obstacles, we can teach your horse to turn on landing having jumped up the bank, and to jump **A** on an angle, or land and jump on a curve three strides going downhill at **B**. You can create a gymnastic which is quite similar to exercise 8 (on page 68) which can be jumped in both directions.

All of these gymnastics will teach your horse to be flexible, land in balance, and wait for you to determine the direction and the striding.

The variation in gymnastic exercises around banks is limited only by your imagination and the level of training that you wish to achieve with your horse. If you first rehearse your horse over rails on the ground, you will be surprised at the complexity of the exercise that you can build for your horse once he understands the nature of the problem.

As the height of the obstacles at **A** and **B** increase, it may be necessary to increase the distance between the bank and **B**. This is quite acceptable. Just watch your horse's reactions carefully and adjust the distance according to the situation. The distances given between **A** and **B** work well on level ground. However, if the bank is on a slope or if there is a permanent log at the top of the bank this may change the nature of the exercise, and again, you should adjust the distances between the portable elements accordingly.

Gymnastic exercise 17 (fold out pages 100 and 101)

Ditches are a necessary part of your horse's education, especially if you are going to foxhunt or event him. Green horses can be trained to jump ditches easily, but you should make sure that you have an experienced older horse present who can give your novice a lead if necessary. Before jumping a formal ditch find a gentle swale in a field somewhere and take three rustic rails to that location. Put two of the rails down in the middle of the swale on the ground approximately 24ins (60cm) apart with the third rail diagonally across them. Then trot back and forth over this, gradually increasing the spread to 3ft (90cm).

If you can find a swale next to a very small revetted ditch this is even better as the horse seems to transfer his attention from one to the other without too much trouble. By all means use a lead, and approach at the canter at first. When jumping the simulated ditch be quite vigorous. If necessary, make your horse walk through the exercise even if you have to be very aggressive with your aids.

Ditches are really a question of obedience, rather than a question of jumping ability, and you should treat them as such. Once your horse is going back and forth over the simulated ditch give him a lead with a

Gymnastic exercise 17
Distance

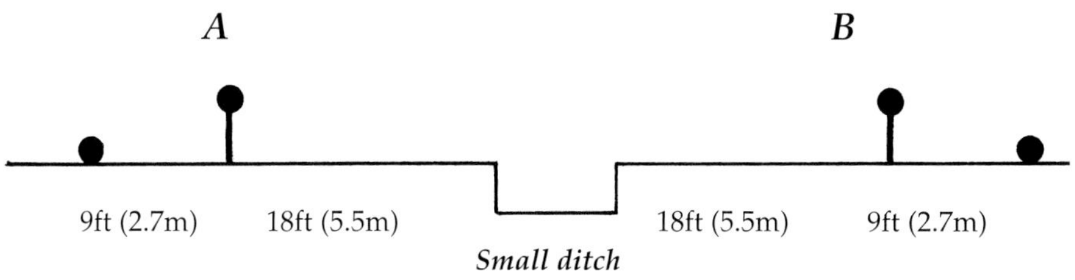

Gymnastic exercise 17 Sequence

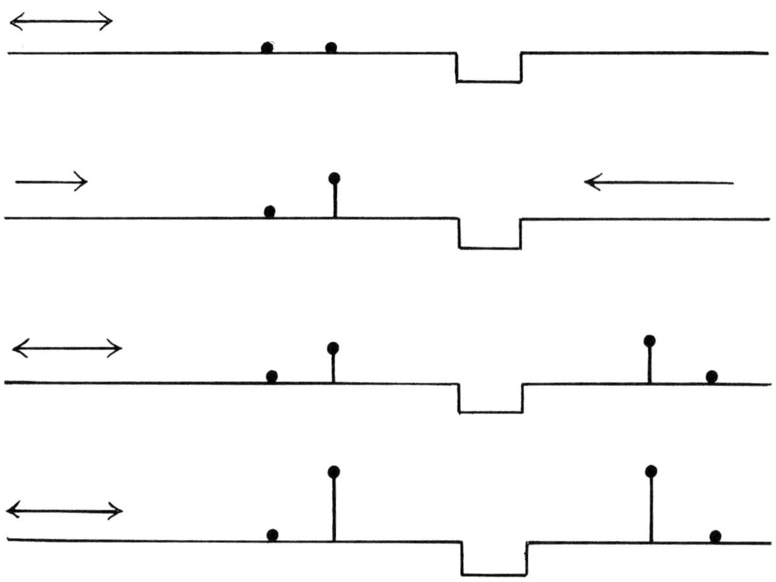

more experienced horse, back and forth over a small natural ditch. Then send your horse back and forth over the ditch at the canter on his own until you are positive that he is confident about the situation.

Now put a rail on the ground 18ft (5.5m) away from the ditch and canter back and forth over this exercise. Once your horse is confident about the ditch you can build the exercise shown at **A** with a 9ft (2.7m) placing pole to quite a small vertical. Trot in over the 9ft (2.7m) rail, jump the small vertical and make sure that your horse takes one stride in jumping the ditch. Then turn around, canter back through the open standards where **B** is going to be placed in a moment, jump the ditch, land, take one stride and jump out over **A** the other way. As your horse gains confidence you can raise the obstacle at **A** until it is quite respectable. My preliminary event horses jump this exercise at 3ft 6ins (1.06m) using these distances over a ditch which is probably 3ft (90cm) in width. When your horse has shown that he understands, you can build an obstacle at **B** again with a 9ft (2.7m) placing rail behind. You can now proceed to trot back and forth from **A** to **B** and **B** to **A**. This simulates a coffin, which is a normal question to find when going across country. Again, the difficulty of the exercise can be increased by increasing the height of the fences at **A** and **B**.

Once your horse is confirmed in understanding a basic coffin type of exercise the same remarks as for exercise 16 apply in so far as the variations on this theme are endless and bounded only by your ingenuity. For example, more experienced horses should be able to jump a vertical fence 10ft (3m) from the edge of the ditch and bounce over the ditch. Extremely experienced horses should be able to bounce, land, and bounce again. Thus the distance between **A** and **B** would be 10ft (3m) on either side of the ditch.

Further possibilities are jumping on an angle across the ditch to rails before and after, and/or jumping a narrow obstacle over the ditch. The high level horses should practise narrow bounces, as this sort of fence is becoming increasingly popular at the intermediate and advanced levels of eventing.

Gymnastic exercise 18 (fold out pages 104 and 105)
Horses should be introduced to water with the same degree of caution that you used in teaching them to jump ditches. If you give your horse a bad experience in his formative stages you will have a hard time with him later on in his career when fences of this nature become more difficult. Horses that are going to be show jumpers should not undertake this, because you do not ever want a show jumper to think it is permissible to step into water. Also for this reason you will rarely find water jumps in the show-jumping phase of an event these days because it is felt to be unfair to ask the horse to jump over water after having just asked him to jump into the water during the cross-country phase.

I prefer a water jump that has at least one end at which the horse can walk in and out without a jumping effort. It is ***absolutely essential*** that the water is shallow and that the footing is level and firm underneath the surface. Jumping into water is a great test of your horse's courage and of his confidence in you, and these are traits that you must treasure and protect.

If the size of the water jump will allow, walk your horse through it following a more experienced horse. Then follow the lead horse through at the trot. Once your horse is relaxed and clearly understands the question, then walk and trot through the water without a lead. Your horse's confidence is your main concern during this lesson because that will be the main question posed by water jumps throughout his competitive career.

Your horse will jump more willingly from the water back to dry ground than he will from dry ground down into the water, so it is better to rehearse in this direction first. Make sure that your horse trots and canters willingly down the slope into the water towards the bank and out onto dry land, before attempting to jump from the bank into the water. Do not add further obstacles until you are convinced that your horse is confident about the question being asked and that he is enjoying the experience.

Having made sure that your horse is confident about the water, you can now proceed as you did in exercise 16 for the dry bank (page 92). Put a rail on the ground 18ft (5.5m) away from the lip of the bank and a placing pole 9ft (2.7m) before that. Then trot in over the placing pole,

Gymnastic exercise 18
Distance

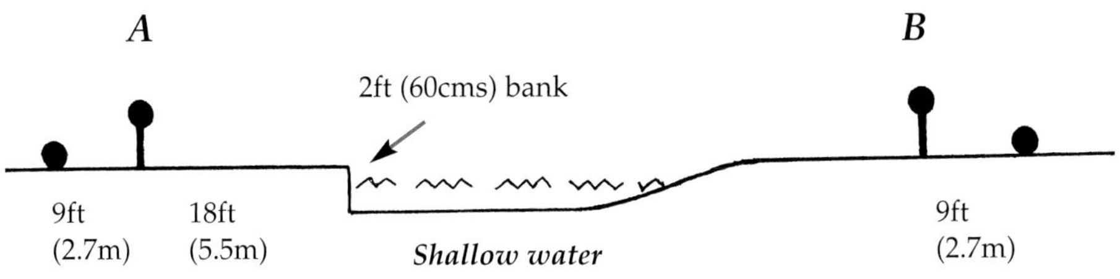

Gymnastic exercise 18
Sequence

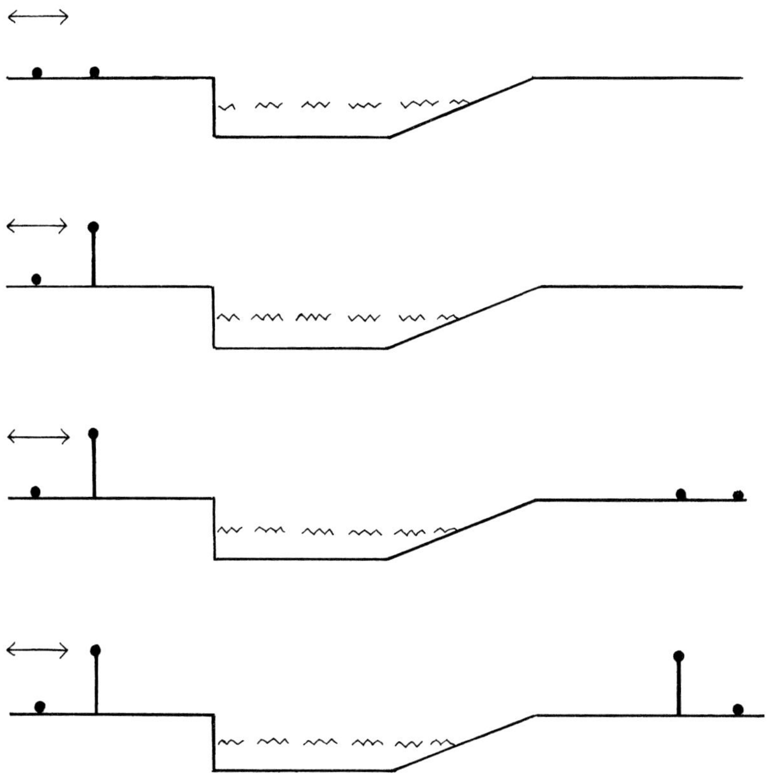

land, make sure that your horse stays in the canter down into the water, continues through the water and canters back out to dry land. Then raise the rail at **A** to 2ft (60cm) in height, and continue.

Afterwards, you can turn around and canter back, jumping from the water back up to dry land and out over the obstacle at **A**. Once your horse handles this easily, you can then place another obstacle on the level at the other end of the water jump as at **B**. It is difficult for me to specify an exact distance without seeing the actual water jump that is going to be used. Generally, you should place the obstacle at **B** on a series of strides that will produce a comfortable if not slightly forward striding for your horse. As your horse gains confidence you can move the obstacle at **B** closer to the water until the horse is jumping **A**, landing, taking a stride, jumping down into the water, cantering through the water, and then jumping from the water out over an obstacle at **B**, landing back on dry land.

The same comments apply now to the water as to bank and ditch exercises; the trainer can vary to an incredible degree the questions that are being asked. Obstacles can be placed in the water so that your horse must jump from the water, landing back in the water. Your long-suffering ground person will need a pair of rubber boots for this exercise. You can create bounces, narrow fences , corners and turning questions depending on the nature of the problem that you want your horse to learn how to solve.

If you are going to go eventing or foxhunting with your horse, it is a good idea to travel around your countryside and see what kind of problems will be posed not just by the water complexes but by the ditches, banks, and so on. Then come home and develop your own gymnastics which will teach your horse how to handle that sort of problem easily and confidently.

Gymnastic exercise 19 (page 108)

In my opinion, cross-country course designers these days are over using the question of narrows and corners, and ignoring the infinite possibilities of terrain. However, our training must prepare our horses for these questions, because it is almost a certainty that you will meet one of these obstacles at your next event.

Although narrow jumps are not exactly gymnastic fences as we have been describing them, narrow jumps are such a useful exercise that I have included a section on their presentation and training. Straightness and balance are so interrelated that the lessons learned here can be applied back to the gymnastic jumping and vice versa.

Place two rails together as shown in the first sequence of exercise 19. I call this exercise the 'to-and-fro rails'. Measure 40ft (12.1m) from the ends of the inside rails and 50ft (15.2m) to the outside of the rails, thus producing two fences on angles to each other. You can jump them individually to get your horse accustomed to them and then begin the exercise. Riding at the canter, approach **A** so that your line of approach and your line of departure are straight to the centre line of the exercise but not perpendicular to either **A** or **B**. Many riders have trouble with this concept at first. Keep in mind that your line of approach and departure should remain straight; it is the jumps that are crooked.

In order to help you with this, place rails on the ground in between **A** and **B** which are parallel to that line. Do not put them too close together as it may cause your horse to dwell in his jumping motion. Ground rails too close together in the landing area can make a horse feel a bit claustrophobic about his landing. The distance from centre to centre of **A** and **B** should produce three quiet strides. You will soon notice that if you deviate in either direction, you will get either two-and-a-half or three-and-a-half strides depending on which way you lost your straightness. Practise going back and forth between **A** and **B** until you can hold an absolutely straight line.

If your horse consistently drifts one way or another, you must correct this before making the exercise more difficult. For example, if your horse continually jumps to the left you must keep your left leg at the girth at the instant of his take-off, open your right rein slightly and press against the neck with your left rein thus keeping your horse straight. One of the most common errors in riding is to attempt to straighten your horse by pulling on the rein rather than by pushing with your leg. Push your horse straight, do not try to pull him straight.

Once you have become adept at maintaining a straight line from **A** to **B** you can add the third rail at **C**. Practise going back and forth until this exercise becomes quite easy for you. As a means of increasing the

Gymnastic exercise 19
Distance

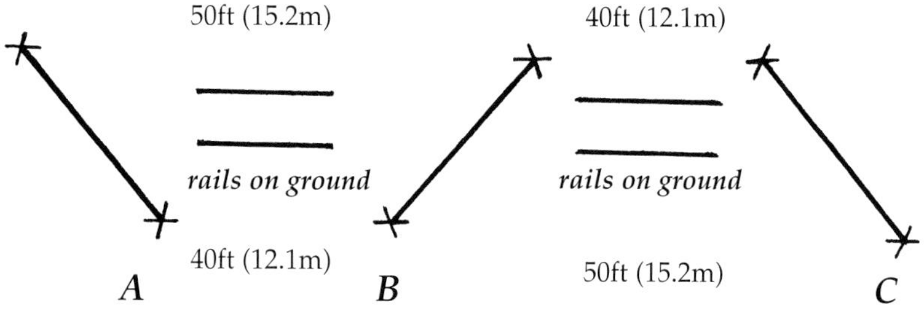

difficulty, you can raise the three rails as you go along, and at some point you should remove the rails on the ground and practise riding your horse on a straight line without visual aids.

To continue your horse's education in jumping on a straight, balanced line, place a vertical fence on the centre line of the arena and take an extra pair of post standards placing them one on either side of the rail as shown in Fig 12(a), below. If you place both extra standards on the same side of the vertical it has the effect of forming a solid obstacle when jumped from the vertical against the extra standards. As a safety factor, I prefer that the fence be able to be knocked down, in case you or your horse makes a mistake.

The opening between the extra standards should be quite sizable at first. Gradually, you should decrease the opening until it is only

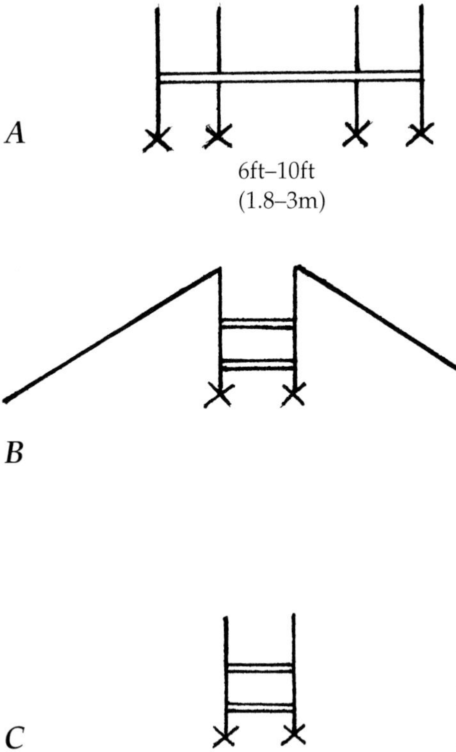

Fig 12. Introducing a narrow fence
a) the first stage
b) with wings
c) without wings.

6ft (1.8m) wide. Horses seem to understand this quite easily and you will be surprised at the progress you can make, and at the narrow size of the opening that your horse will jump through willingly.

Once your horse jumps a narrow opening you can build in-and-outs and gymnastics on related distances using extra standards to produce a narrower and narrower opening for your horse to negotiate. A 6ft (1.8m) opening is the smallest opening you should ask your horse to jump through.

The next step is to take rails that are approximately 6ft (1.8m) in length and build a small vertical. Put a wing on either side of the narrow jump, which will frame the fence in an attractive manner for your horse as in Fig 12b. Trot and canter back and forth until your horse is relaxed jumping over the narrow rails and then you can raise the rails to increase the difficulty.

Once you feel confident about this you can remove the wings from the narrow jump, Fig 12c. However you should lower the rails at first until you are sure your horse is trustworthy. If he starts to swerve to one side or the other you are better off to replace the wings until your horse willingly remains straight in the approach and the departure.

Corners

If your horse is comfortable and confident over narrow jumps at the trot and the canter, it is time to introduce him to corners.

Corners should be viewed as an opportunity, not a problem. By this I mean that in the cross-country phase of an event, corners usually provide an opportunity to jump one obstacle rather than several. In all aspects of jumping they should be viewed as jumping a narrow oxer rather than jumping a wider oxer.

Look back at the 'to-and-fro' rails that you jumped over first when beginning to teach your horse to jump multiple angled obstacles on a straight line (page 108). If you imagine dotted lines coming down from the rails at **A** and **B**, at some point they would intersect to form a corner. So when you jumped **A** and **B**, you rehearsed jumping over the front rail of the corner, then you were allowed to take three strides, and then jumped out over the back part of the corner. If you used slightly less distance you could do this on two strides and then one stride.

Then you could jump an angled bounce at some point over that imaginary rail. Although I do not recommend it, it is possible.

Finally, if you moved your imaginary line of approach far enough, you would jump the front and the back rail of the exercise in one as you do over a corner fence. If you draw this exercise on graph paper, you should notice that your line of approach and departure remains parallel as you move up and down through this imaginary grid.

Corners are easy to jump if you are accurate in your alignment. We cannot jump corners successfully by approaching perpendicular to the front rail as that increases the spread to a dramatic degree. Nor can we approach perpendicular to the back rail because that invites your horse to run out toward the single post standard. So we should imagine a third rail higher than the two rails forming the corner, which bisects the angle of the corner. We then approach on a line that is perpendicular to that imaginary rail. This has the effect of splitting the difference in the angles and allows you to ride on a straight line over the corner as shown in Fig 13 below.

If the corner is, for example, a left point (which means that the two rails of the corner come together at the left side of the fence) you should not make the mistake of riding from right to left but rather make the mistake of riding a tiny bit back from left to right, jumping the smaller part of the spread.

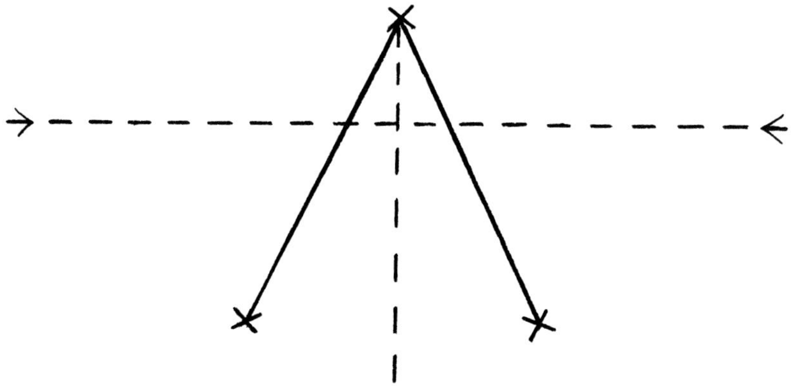

Fig 13. An imaginary third rail bisects the angle of a corner fence.

Introduce your horse to corners by building the three standards as shown in Fig 14 below and then put the front rail of the corner down so that it is merely an attractive ground line to a vertical fence. Gradually move the front rail forward until it is on the ground next to the standard. The distance between the two outside standards should be about 4ft (1.2m) at first. Later on you can increase this distance to 9ft (2.7m) which will truly give you and your horse the sensation of jumping a corner.

If your horse understands this exercise you can now raise the front rail up into the cups, making sure that the back rail of the corner is slightly higher than the front rail just as you would with a round oxer. If you have trouble visualising your alignment have the ground person place an extra rail at the intersection of the two rails of the corner and visualise

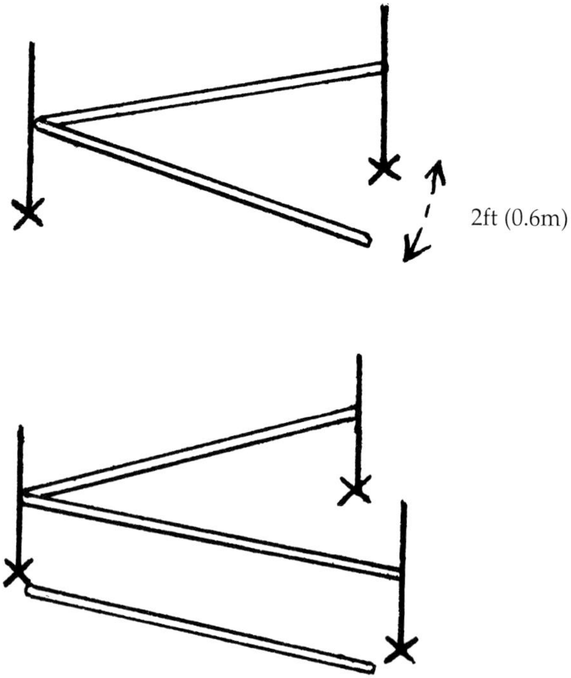

Fig 14. Using normal standards and poles, the two stages of introducing a corner fence.

your approach to that guideline. Then have the ground person take the rail away and approach on that line at the canter.

Once your horse is consistently jumping corners well, you should begin to jump corners in combination. Be careful with the alignments of the two corners, so as to promote a straight line over the narrowest parts of the corners.

Jump the combination 24ft (7.3m), 36ft (11m) or 48ft (14.6m) with the corners pointing the same way at first, and then later on with the corners opposed, that is a left point corner, followed by a right point corner. This is a serious test of straightness, since if your horse has any tendency to drift, a spread will make it worse, and he may run out or canter past the second corner. If you can jump opposed corners 36ft (11m) apart at the height of your competitive level you can be well pleased with your state of training.

7

Exercises for Correcting Errors

It is inevitable in the training of any horse that problems in specific areas may develop. If your horse continually makes an error, you should analyse what he is doing wrong and set up exercises which will help teach him what it is that you want him to do.

Running out

Refusals or 'run outs' are some of the most common jumping mistakes you will come across during the training of your horse.

If your horse continually runs out to the left, the simplest means of correction is to put an additional rail on top of the standard, as shown in Fig 15 below. Do not put this rail in a cup because if your horse jumps off to the side badly and hits the wing, it has the effect of fixing the rail in the ground. If the rail is on top of the post it will be easily dislodged.

Of course, horses who deviate this violently should have their

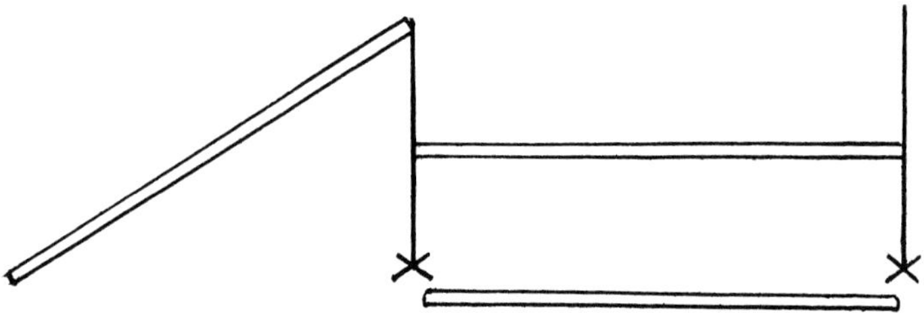

Fig 15. A rail positioned like this will discourage running out.

dressage work increased and improved, to refine their sensitivity to your aids on that side. In addition, horses of this nature benefit from work over narrow fences and corners such as those described at the end of exercise 19.

Drifting

A horse who jumps but swerves across the fence, landing on a different line from the one on which he took off, is said to be 'drifting'. Your horse does this because he is pushing more with one hind leg than another and landing with the weight more on one shoulder than the other. If your horse jumps to the left you should emphasise left shoulder-in and right turn on the haunches in order to put your horse's body more into alignment. As with most jumping problems, work on the flat is the first place to start.

The simplest and most effective means I have ever found of straightening horses that drift while jumping is to put a half cross rail up behind a normal vertical, as shown in Fig 16 below. Place the half cross rail behind the vertical and allow the width of the rail between the obstacle and the half cross rail so that if your horse hits the vertical rail, there is room for it to fall out of the cup. (Do not place the half cross rail in a cup at the top of the standard; it causes the fence to be fixed in nature, and you want the rail to become dislodged should your horse make a mistake.)

Other means of correcting a horse who drifts are to place a rail on the ground in front of and after the fence. This will help some horses, although I have not found it to be as efficient as the half cross rail. Another means of correction is to jump on a circle in the opposite direction. For example, if

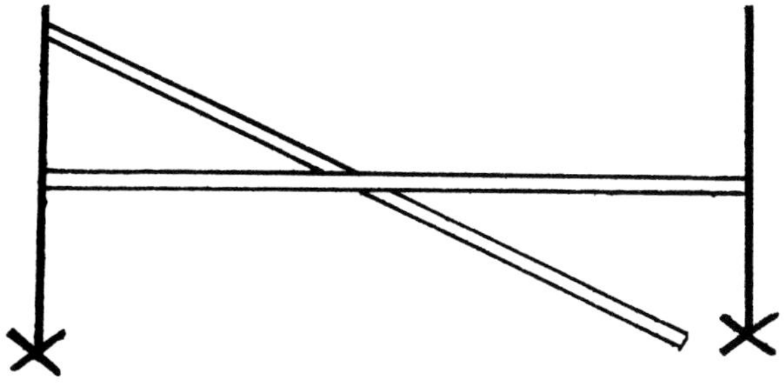

Fig 16. The half cross rail discourages drifting.

your horse continually lands to the left you should circle to the right and teach the horse to jump back the other way across the obstacle.

Rushing

The most common fault in training a horse to jump is that the horse begins to anticipate and rush his fences. Therefore you need to have a wide range of tools available to you in order to deal with this problem. If your horse starts to rush we can go back to exercise 5 on page 50, which is an excellent exercise to teach your horse to wait. The double bounce used in this exercise has the effect of training your horse not to over commit himself because there are obstacles at the end of the line which will make him continue to compress his stride. If your horse is beginning to rush, revisit exercise 5 and see if that helps.

Gymnastic exercise 20 (fold out page 118)

This exercise which is quite simple will also serve to calm a rushing horse. Build eight small jumps on the corner as illustrated, to form a box with open sides. The size of the box should be 80ft (24.3m) from corner to corner both ways.

Warm your horse up over a few individual fences and then canter him on a circle inside the box. You have a choice of four fences which you can jump on either lead. Do not jump any of them until the horse is settled and remains on the circle. Then leave the circle and jump a fence. At first you can land on the lead of your horse's choosing, but later on you should begin to select the lead for your horse. To do this, review the aids you used in exercise 8 (page 65), when you first taught your horse to change leads and direction over a fence.

Landing after the fence with a horse who is rushing will usually be a fairly enthusiastic production, and you should immediately turn back into the box and continue the circle. It may take several revolutions around the circle before the horse settles again. Do not jump again until you have re-established your horse's calmness. You can increase the difficulty of this exercise by jumping into the circle over an obstacle and cantering around that circle until your horse is calm and balanced again.

Work in both directions until you have eventually jumped all eight fences from the canter. This exercise takes some time to work but it is effective as long as you are dedicated to re-establishing your horse's balance and mental discipline after each fence before continuing to jump.

Gymnastic exercise 21 (fold out page 119)

For exercise 21, you will need two verticals and two oxers which should be placed in an arena as shown. If you do not have an enclosed area you can put extra standards at the measured distances to give you a reference as to the size and shape of the curves that you will describe while doing this exercise. However, the exercise will work best in an indoor school or a well fenced arena.

The purpose of exercise 21 is to make your horse more rideable around a course, by teaching him not to 'pop', or 'fall in', in other words, lean over his inside shoulder at the end of the arena.

Start out with one obstacle placed at **A** in the illustration. Canter on the left hand through the open standards at **B** jumping **A** at a low height, 2ft–2ft 6ins (60–75cm). Turn left into the wall, re-establish the left canter lead, continue left down the long side and then again turn left through the open standards at **B** and jump **A**, again turning left. You should continue this until your horse anticipates the turn back into the corner and lands in balance, hopefully on the left lead.

Then move to the other side of the arena and do the same thing on the right lead. Canter through the open standards at **D,** jumping a small vertical at **C** and turning to the right at the corner. Continue down the long side, turn back to the right through the open standards at **D** and so on. Just as with the first obstacle on the left lead you should continue this until your horse begins to anticipate turning back into the wall, and lands on the right lead.

Then you can, for example, start out on the left lead down the long side, turning back towards **A**, jumping, and landing on the left lead. Continue on the left lead turning then through the open standards at **D** and jumping the small obstacle at **C,** landing on the right lead.

Repeat this variation of a 'figure eight' exercise several times and then walk.

While you and your horse catch your breath, have your ground person put a small oxer at **B** and **D**. Then repeat the exercise as before,

Gymnastic exercise 20
Distance

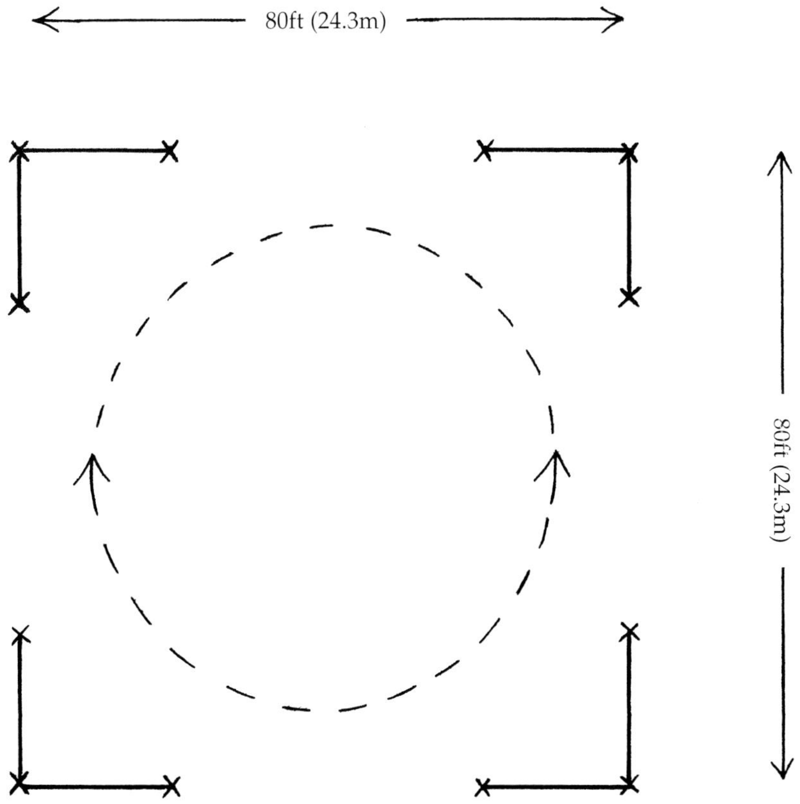

Gymnastic exercise 21
Distance

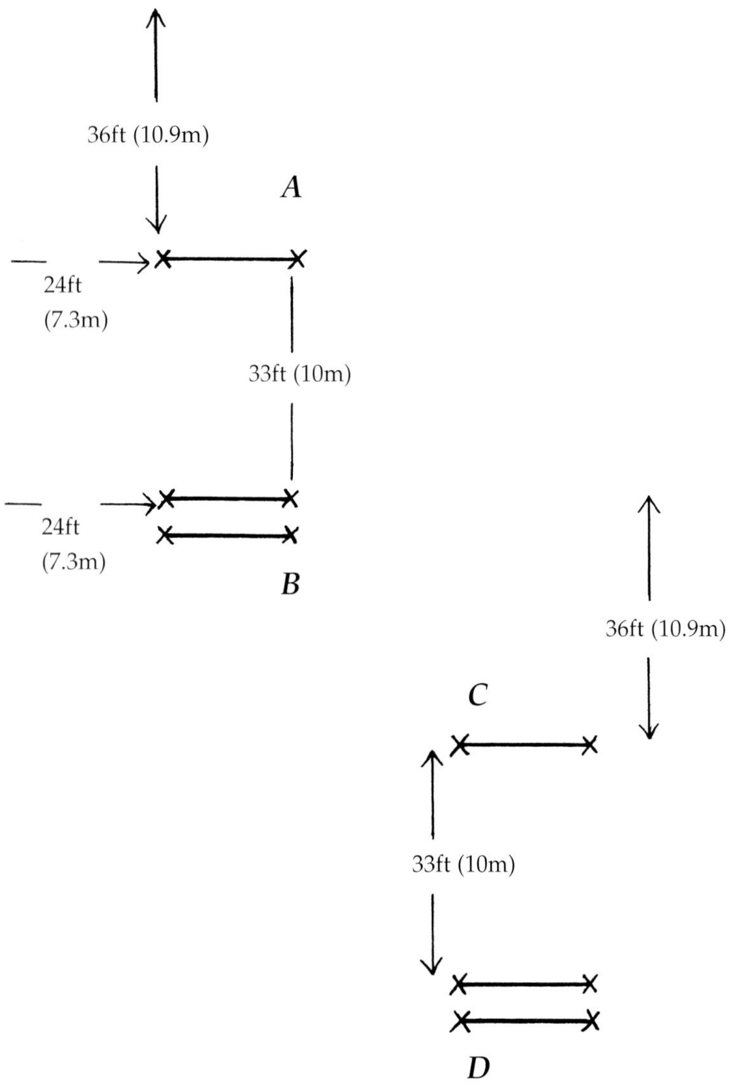

beginning on the left lead, turning back, jumping the oxer at **B**, taking two quiet strides, jumping the vertical at **A** and turning left. Repeat this several times, then take another break.

Resume work, this time on the right lead, and jump from **D** to **C** in two strides, turning right after **C** and so on. Again, after several repetitions, take a break.

Later on, you can vary this exercise slightly. For example, on the right lead you can approach from the wall towards **A**, landing on the left lead, turning back into the wall and approaching on an angle to **B**. After **B** turn back to the right on the right lead and jump **A** on an angle again and so on.

After the horse figures this out, take another break and do the same 'figure eight' exercise between **C** and **D**. Begin on the left lead approaching from between the wall and the oxer at **D** and jump the small vertical at **C**. Land on the right lead turning out of the corner to approach the oxer at **D** on a slight left to right angle, land after **D** and turn back to **C**, and so on.

The wall has a powerful effect on horses that want to rush. To execute the turns, you should use the same aids as you did during exercises 8 and 9 (pages 65 and 70).

Gymnastic exercise 22 (page 121)

Changing leads

Sometimes the simplest exercises are the best. Place four jumps on the centre line of your arena as shown. **A** and **B**, and **C** and **D.** should be at right angles to each other. Have at least 75ft (22.8m) between the points of the two joined fences and place a single post standard at least 85ft (25.9m) away from the point between **A** and **B**.

Start in canter over **A** on the left lead. When you land continue behind **D** and **C** on the right lead and approach **B**. Make sure that you are perpendicular to **B** and that when you land you continue straight for a few strides. Pass behind the post standard on the centre line and re-approach **A** on the left lead. Continue along this 'figure eight' path for several repetitions then walk, give your horse a break and resume work on the right lead.

Now your path will go as follows: approaching **B** from beyond the

Gymnastic exercise 22
Distance

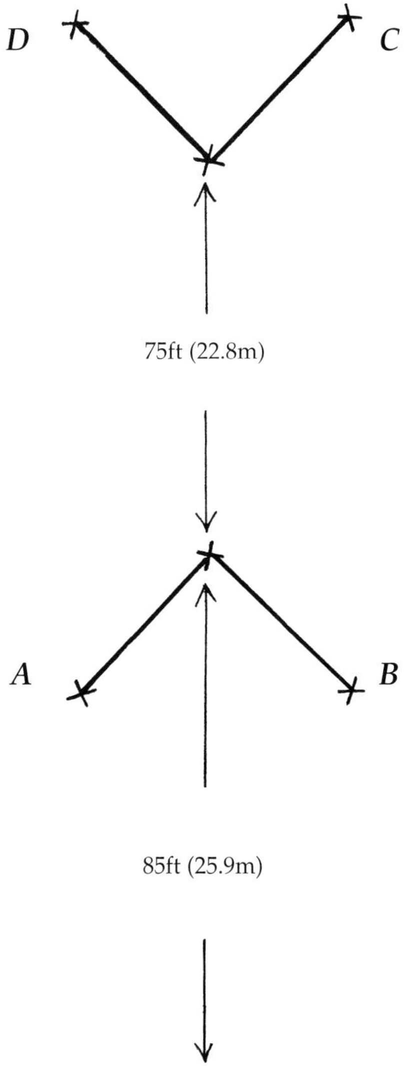

post standard in right lead canter, jump **B** and land on the left lead. Continue behind **C** and **D** on the left lead, controlling your curve until your approach is perpendicular to jump **A**. Land on the right lead, continue behind the post standard and resume the figure eight. Again you should stay on this figure eight until your horse is relaxed and changes leads over each jump. If you have trouble with this you should refer back to the 'clover leaf' pattern, which is exercise 8 on page 65, and review the aids necessary for changing lead over the jumps.

Once your horse has settled in there are several variations that you can make using this same basic pattern. For example, approach **A** on the left lead. This time turn inside of **D** and **C** and continue on a curve back to **B**. Landing after **B** you should turn back to the left inside the single post standard and continue on a curve back again to **A**. Remember to keep the curve at the top and the bottom of the arena symmetrical so that as you leave the turn you are once again perpendicular to the next fence.

If your horse has mastered this exercise you can start to jump, for example, from **A** to **D** back to **B** and then from **A** straight ahead, turning right back to **C** and continuing on a curve back to **B.** and so on.

There are any number of possible permutations and combinations available to you, but the key aspect is that your horse should land after each jump at the same speed with which you approached it. Strive for a clock-like regularity in the approach and in the departure from these obstacles.

Exercises for horses who slow down in the take-off

If your horse 'stalls' or is sticky at the moment of take-off, you should first of all view this as a dressage problem. Your horse should land going at the same speed that he takes off. If he gradually slows through your gymnastic exercises, your horse is getting behind your leg and a sharp prod with a spur or a quick reminder with a stick directly behind your leg will usually solve the problem.

Gymnastic exercise 23 (pages 125 and 126)

If you continue to have difficulty, set up exercise 23 as shown opposite and practise through it several times. First of all, trot your horse over the placing rail 9ft (2.7m) away from a small vertical until at **A** you feel he is warmed up. Then build the oxer at **B** and trot through again taking two strides from **A** to **B**. This distance will be slightly forward and you will have to keep your legs on in order not to have your horse 'chip in' a third stride. When your horse is landing and taking the correct number of strides to **B** then build a triple bar at **C**, 42ft (12.8m) away as shown.

This exercise will now produce a rhythm of trot in, jump the vertical, land and take two strides, jumping the oxer at **B**. Concentrate on landing behind **B** going forward. Press your horse forward for three strides and jump the triple bar. Remember to keep your leg on at the point of take-off over **C** so that your horse stretches out over the triple bar and lands with the same speed that he took off. Several applications of this exercise may be necessary in order to get your horse to begin to move his stride up. As a general comment do not ask your horse to lengthen his stride for more than three strides at a time or you will find that your horse will begin to 'sprawl' and go on his forehand.

Another exercise which may be worthwhile to help keep your horse from 'stalling' is to use ground lines both in front of and behind your obstacles. Make sure that the ground line in front of the obstacle is at least the height of the fence away from the fence, if not more, and certainly on the landing side the ground line should be 6ins–1ft (15–30cm) more than the height of the fence behind the fence. This will cause your horse to reach out more with his shoulders for the landing, thus taking a longer stride in the recovery phase.

Tips for improving horses who knock fences down in front

Horses who hang their front legs are difficult to train. However, they can be improved. I personally do not rap or pole my horses because event horses have to go across country first, and by the time you get to the show jumping phase, your horse has usually forgotten all about his experiences of a week or so ago.

I find that by jumping low wide oxers and jumping longer

Fig 17. The horse whose hind legs are not engaged will find it more difficult to jump clean (top); whereas the horse who rocks back onto his quarters finds it easier to 'snap up' with his knees (above).

distances, I can teach the horse to draw his shoulder up and forward. I work over longer distances first and try to stretch the horse's shoulders out, and then I work the horse back into shorter and shorter distances, with increasingly higher obstacles. The reason I do it this way is because I have found that if you compress the distance between obstacles first, for a horse who is dangling his forehand, invariably you will cause him to jump higher but to dangle worse. Your horse has

Gymnastic exercise 23
Distance

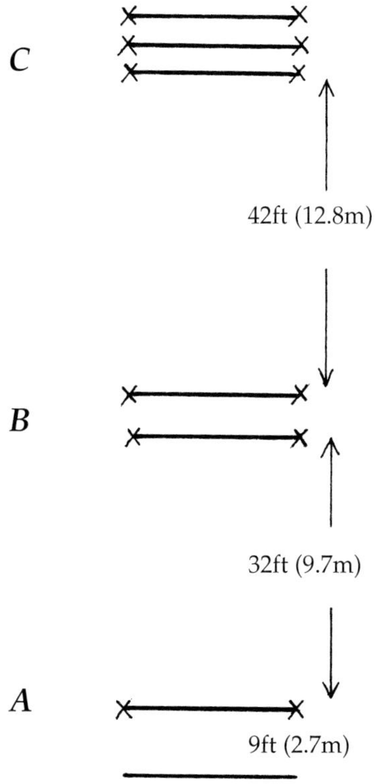

Gymnastic exercise 23
Sequence

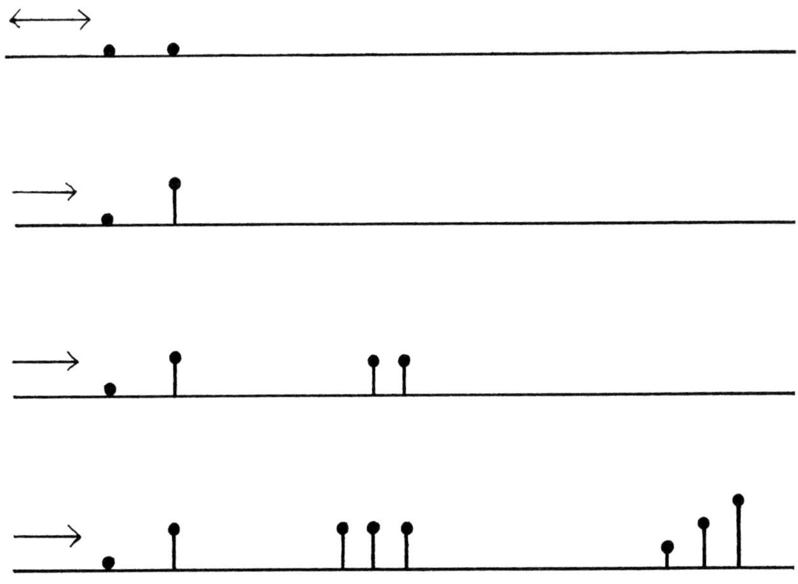

trouble 'snapping' his knees because he has not rocked back on his hindquarters (see Fig 17). You must increase the swing of the hindquarters first which will elevate the forehand, which will then cause the horse to become more efficient in his shoulders.

There is a direct correlation between my comments here and classical dressage theory. Go forward first, then compress.

Knocking down fences behind

Occasionally you will deal with horses who are a bit slow behind. Work this sort of horse through double bounce oxers. Low oxers 3ft (90cm) high and 3ft (90cm) wide set 12ft (3.6m) apart from the next oxer, and again 12ft (3.6m) apart from the next oxer, will many times cause the horse to follow through better with his hindquarters. Alternatively, an obstacle which will help is illustrated in Fig 18. Rest two extra rails in an 'A' shape over a medium sized vertical and canter your horse over the point of the 'A'. Gradually move the point of the 'A' back behind the vertical, taking care to make sure that your horse jumps straight over the point of the 'A'. Usually he will bump the 'A' once with his hind feet and then start to make a better effort. You may have to move the point of the 'A' further beyond the vertical to have an effect on your horse.

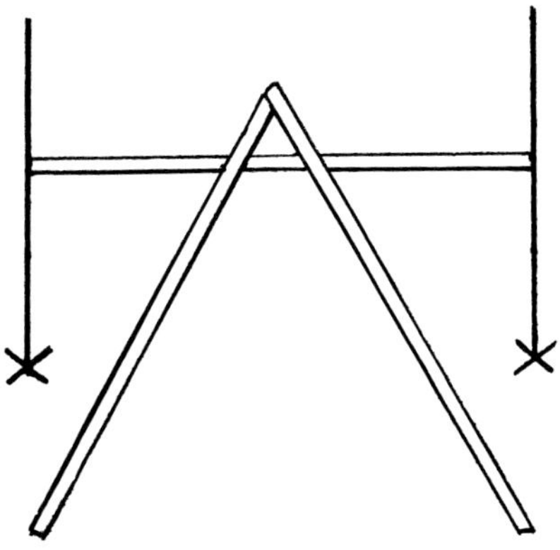

Fig 18. An 'A' frame fence.

8

Conclusion

I hope that you have enjoyed this book and that your horse has improved his performance over jumps. A few reminders are in order here to conclude this work, and to provide you with a quick reminder in the future.

- ❑ Calm, forward and straight are all the rules for training horses you will ever need.
- ❑ When jumping, place your weight over your horse' s shoulders and soften your reins. You will transform a dull slave into a joyful and willing partner.
- ❑ You will make better progress if you jump little and often.
- ❑ Keep the obstacles small until you are sure your horse understands the question you are asking. Once he understands, his God-given talent is the only real limit.
- ❑ Teach your horse new skills by breaking those skills down into their most basic components.
- ❑ Time spent on improving your own jumping position is never wasted. There is a strong relationship between how you ride and how your horse goes. To improve your horse, improve your self.
- ❑ Deal with your horse's mistakes as lack of knowledge, rather than

wilful disobedience. Determine which part of the question your horse does not understand, and develop a way to explain it to him. I am sure he will respond and improve.

- ❑ As you go along in riding, you will develop your own system of training horses. Keep in mind the preface to the U.S. Army *Manual of Equitation*, 1921 edition, which says that any system of training which destroys the tranquillity of horses is defective.

A close partnership with a horse is one of the greatest pleasures known to mankind. I hope this book helps you to attain that partnership.

Bibliography

I hope you are interested enough in improving your own and your horse's performance to read further. Certainly people cannot learn how to ride without ever reading a book on the subject. Your progress will be much faster, and your eventual results will be much better, if you study the basics of your sport.

You will find here a list of books on jumping, in the order that they appear on my library shelf. They made a great deal of sense to me when I read them, so much so that I wrote a book on the topic myself, which I include here.

I am sure your riding will improve if you apply some of the lessons to be learned from these books.

The de Némethy Method, Bertalan de Némethy
Doubleday 1988

Riding and Jumping, William Steinkraus
Doubleday 1961

Reflections on Riding and Jumping, William Steinkraus
Doubleday 1991

Riding and Schooling Horses, Col. Harry D. Chamberlin
Derrydale 1934

Training Hunters, Jumpers and Hacks, Col. Harry D. Chamberlin
Derrydale 1937

Training Showjumpers, Anthony Paalman
J. A. Allen 1998

Hunter Seat Equitation, George H. Morris
Doubleday 1971

Winning with Frank Chapot, Frank Chapot
Breakthrough Publications 1992
Ann Kursinski's Riding and Jumping Clinic, Ann Kursinski
Doubleday 1995
Jumping is Jumping, Jane Wallace
Methuen 1994
Training the Three Day Event Horse and Rider, James C. Wofford
Doubleday 1995

Personal Notes and Comments

Personal Notes and Comments

I wish to order the following books:

Number of copies/Title/Price

....

....

....

....

Total books.......... ***Total £*** ....

Please make cheques out to **Compass Equestrian Ltd**., or fill in your VISA/MASTERCARD details below. *P&P free (UK)*

Name: *(please print)*

....

Address: ....

....

....

....

....

Signature: ....

VISA/MASTERCARD no: ....
Expiry
date:...